SPIRITUAL WRITINGS

SPIRITUAL WRITINGS

Selected Poems and Prose

Samuel Taylor Coleridge

Introduction by Robert Van de Weyer

Fount

An Imprint of HarperCollinsPublishers

Fount Paperbacks is an Imprint of
\HarperCollins*Religious*
Part of HarperCollins*Publishers*
77–85 Fulham Palace Road, London W6 8JB

First published in Great Britain
in 1997 by Fount Paperbacks

1   3   5   7   9   10   8   6   4   2

Copyright in the Introduction © 1997
by Robert Van de Weyer

A catalogue record for this book is
available from the British Library

ISBN 0 00 628 032 3

Printed and bound in Great Britain by
Caledonian International Book Manufacturing Ltd, Glasgow

Contents

Introduction

Samuel Taylor Coleridge is remembered by most people as a romantic poet and an opium addict. At that time opium addiction did not carry the social stigma it does today; even the great Evangelical social reformer William Wilberforce shared the habit. More importantly, poetry was only one part of Coleridge's literary output; his greatest and most original influence was as a religious and political thinker – indeed, some have argued that he set the agenda for Christian thought in the nineteenth and twentieth centuries. As the Industrial Revolution spread across Britain and Europe, and as the scientific attitudes of the Enlightenment became universally accepted, Coleridge saw clearly that traditional religious orthodoxy would cease to be viable. He thus posed questions about morality, theology and spirituality which seemed shocking in his day, but are now at the heart of religious debate. And in seeking answers he offered insights which are often astonishing in their depth. It is the mark of a great mind and spirit that even when he is wrong, his errors stimulate fresh thought.

Coleridge was born in 1772 in a Devonshire village where his father was vicar and schoolmaster. When he was nine his father died, and his mother was forced to send him to a charitable boarding school. Coleridge hated the savage school discipline, but his quick wit attracted the attention of the more cultured masters, who taught him to enjoy intellectual discussion – a pleasure which in later life carried him through his darkest periods. In 1791 he went up to Jesus College, Cambridge, where he soon attracted a circle of friends who would argue late into the night about the burning issues of the time. The French Revolution had only just begun, and its high ideals caught the youthful imagination of Coleridge and his companions. But already his private affairs were collapsing into chaos. He was accumulating large debts, and he began to take opium to relieve him of rheumatic pains and to help him to sleep. He was also falling behind in his studies because his restless mind was unable to concentrate on the work his tutors set. His debts, and his imminent academic failure, so alarmed him that in 1794 he fled Cambridge, took a false name, and joined the army. When his friends realized what had happened, they raised money to pay for his discharge.

The next eight years saw the first flowering of his genius. In 1795 the publisher Joseph Cottle introduced him to William Wordsworth; this led to the appearance three years later of *Lyrical Ballads*, one of the most influential volumes of poetry in the history of the English language. Opening with Coleridge's 'Ancient Mariner', and closing with Wordsworth's 'Tintern Abbey', it was also a manifesto of the Romantic Movement. In the preface and in the poems the two men asserted their faith in the integrity of the human soul, and its unity with the natural order. They saw themselves as reacting against the scientific rationalism of the eighteenth century, which they regarded as spiritually sterile. Instead they wanted, through the medium of poetry, to penetrate the deep mysteries of the psyche. And these mysteries are reflected in the beauty and majesty of nature. Inspired by this vision, Coleridge and Wordsworth wrote poems that are at once profound and immensely enjoyable.

During this eight-year period Coleridge also wrote and lectured prolifically on political and religious subjects. He was a political radical; but already, unlike most of his contemporaries, he could see the moral and spiritual dimension of every political issue. He was appalled not only at the poverty of the new industrial towns, but also at the spiritual degradation of the working class. He opposed the war against France, denouncing the blindness of the politicians and generals who were so obsessed with the glories of war that they failed to notice its innocent victims. Likewise, when he joined

Wilberforce in campaigning for the abolition of slavery, it was not only the physical suffering of the slaves which outraged him, but also the moral deafness of the British upper class whose 'nerves are not shattered by the shrieks' of the slaves, and who calmly 'sip a beverage sweetened with human blood'.

At school, Coleridge had enjoyed talking about religion to any visiting clergyman, and shortly after his escapade in the army he wrote: 'to the cause of Religion I solemnly devote all my best faculties.' Financial necessity forced him briefly to consider becoming a Unitarian minister, but the promise of an annual pension of £150 from the Wedgwood family to support him as a writer enabled him to avoid regular employment. His personal religious quest could never be fitted into an orthodox doctrinal framework, and by 1805 he was writing: 'O, that my mind may be made up as to the character of Jesus and of his historical Christianity' – questions that have subsequently penetrated to the heart of theological debate. Coleridge sought to overcome the problems of theology by making subjective spiritual experience, rather than objective doctrine, the centre of religion: 'Christianity is not a theory, or a speculation, but a Life – not a philosophy of life, but a living process' – words which again foreshadow future religious thought. He came to believe that there was a form of 'reason' higher than intellectual understanding, which he called 'conscience'; and this faculty enabled one to know God directly within the soul, and so to follow the divine moral law. It is through the workings of 'conscience', Coleridge asserted, that people of religious convictions should involve themselves in political issues of justice and freedom.

In committing himself to religion, Coleridge also wished to give his religious and political views practical expression. In 1794, with another young poet, Robert Southey, he conceived a scheme, which they called Pantisocracy, to start an ideal communist society in America, drawing up the most detailed plans. It eventually came to nothing owing to Southey's caution and Coleridge's lack of practical skills. But in the course of preparation Coleridge married

Sara Fricker, another prospective Pantisocrat. He never loved her, and even at the time of their wedding was in love with another woman, Mary Evans; and, although they had three children, their life together was miserable. In 1802 they separated, and the next fourteen years were a period of deepening unhappiness and despair. His opium addiction condemned him to poor health, and his creative genius seemed to be spent. In 1809 he launched a new magazine, but this quickly foundered through lack of funds.

By 1816 his friends feared he would commit suicide, and they persuaded him to visit James Gillman, a doctor in Highgate. A close bond was immediately formed between these two contrasting personalities, the wayward genius and the kindly physician; and Dr Gillman and his wife invited Coleridge to live with them. Coleridge remained there until his death in 1834. Dr Gillman gradually reduced Coleridge's intake of opium; Coleridge found within the Gillman household the domestic peace and order that he had never been able to provide for himself. These later years saw a second flowering of his astonishing intellect. He wrote little poetry, but addressed himself wholly to religion and politics, searching for a vision that would unify the whole of human life.

Coleridge was the first Christian writer to question the ethics of free market capitalism, which was now widely regarded as divinely ordained. He accused the new middle class of idolatry: 'under the specious names of utility and practical knowledge [we] look at all things through the medium of the market', so that even human beings themselves are counted 'by their marketable value'. He did not repudiate the free market, but believed it should be counter-balanced by a stable framework which should be upheld by the State. The centre of this framework should be education, since this would enable people to manage their own affairs – eventually even taking over the factories where they worked.

Coleridge's political concerns led him back to the Bible, especially the Old Testament, which he saw as an invaluable guide to social action. In particular he proposed that the social framework for a modern state should to a great degree follow the Hebrew model. Yet for Coleridge the commitment to God was above his loyalty to any particular religion, including Christianity. He saw himself as 'groaning under a deep sense of infirmity and manifold imperfection', who thus 'feels the want, the necessity, of religious support.' And he declared himself as one 'who loves Truth with an indescribable awe.' This need for support, and this love of Truth, prompted him to seek spiritual insight from every available source. As he concluded near the end of his life, every individual and every society can do no more than 'creep towards the light'.

In 1828 Coleridge was visited by the young Thomas Carlyle, who wrote: 'I reckon him a man of great and useless genius; a strange, not at all a great man.' And even his biographer, Sir Edmund Chambers, concluded that his only legacy was 'a handful of golden poems.' Certainly 'The Ancient Mariner', 'Kubla Khan', 'Frost at Midnight' and the rest remain as popular and highly-regarded as ever. Happily, however, in recent decades critics have begun to rediscover his prose; and the time has undoubtedly come when we should allow ourselves to be disturbed, challenged and, at times, uplifted by his religious writings. It would be wrong to call him a theologian, because his thought is not systematic or logical enough for such a title. Nor was he a mystic. He was a much rarer creature: a prophet – who shared the Hebrew prophets' passion for justice and for truth.

ROBERT VAN DE WEYER

Poems

EPITAPH ON AN INFANT

Ere Sin could blight or Sorrow fade,
    Death came with friendly care;
The opening bud to Heaven conveyed,
    And bade it blossom there.
1790

THE AEOLIAN HARP

My pensive Sara! thy soft cheek reclined
Thus on mine arm, most soothing sweet it is
To sit beside our cot, our cot o'ergrown
With white-flowered jasmine, and the broad-leaved myrtle,
(Meet emblems they of Innocence and Love!)
And watch the clouds, that late were rich with light,
Slow saddening round, and mark the star of eve
Serenely brilliant (such should wisdom be)
Shine opposite! How exquisite the scents
Snatched from yon bean-field! and the world so hushed!
The stilly murmur of the distant sea
Tells us of silence.

                    And that simplest lute,
Placed length-ways in the clasping casement, hark!
How by the desultory breeze caressed,
Like some coy maid half yielding to her lover,
It pours such sweet unbraiding, as must needs
Tempt to repeat the wrong! And now, its strings
Boldlier swept, the long sequacious notes
Over delicious surges sink and rise,
Such a soft floating witchery of sound
As twilight Elfins make, when they at eve
Voyage on gentle gales from Fairy-Land,
Where Melodies round honey-dropping flowers,
Footless and wild, like birds of Paradise,
Nor pause, nor perch, hovering on untamed wing!
O the one life within us and abroad,
Which meets all motion and becomes its soul,
A light in sound, a sound-like power in light,
Rhythm in all thought, and joyance every where –
Methinks, it should have been impossible
Not to love all things in a world so filled;

Where the breeze warbles, and the mute still air
Is Music slumbering on her instrument.

And thus, my love! as on the midway slope
Of yonder hill I stretch my limbs at noon,
Whilst through my half-closed eye-lids I behold
The sunbeams dance, like diamonds, on the main,
And tranquil muse upon tranquillity;
Full many a thought uncalled and undetained,
And many idle flitting phantasies,
Traverse my indolent and passive brain,
As wild and various as the random gales
That swell and flutter on this subject lute!
And what if all of animated nature
Be but organic harps diversely framed,
That tremble into thought, as o'er them sweeps
Plastic and vast, one intellectual breeze,
At once the Soul of each, and God of All?
But thy more serious eye a mild reproof
Darts, O beloved woman! nor such thoughts
Dim and unhallowed dost thou not reject,
And biddest me walk humbly with my God.
Meek daughter in the family of Christ!
Well hast thou said and holily dispraised
These shapings of the unregenerate mind;
Bubbles that glitter as they rise and break
On vain Philosophy's aye-babbling spring.
For never guiltless may I speak of him.
The Incomprehensible! save when with awe
I praise him, and with Faith that inly feels;
Who with his saving mercies healed me,
A sinful and most miserable man,
Wildered and dark, and gave me to possess
Peace, and this cot, and thee, heart-honoured Maid!
1795

TO AN INFANT

Ah! cease thy tears and sobs, my little Life!
I did but snatch away the unclasped knife:
Some safer toy will soon arrest thine eye,
And to quick laughter change this peevish cry!
Poor stumbler on the rocky coast of woe,
Tutor'd by pain each source of pain to know!
Alike the foodful fruit and scorching fire
Awake thy eager grasp and young desire;
Alike the Good, the Ill offend thy sight,
And rouse the stormy sense of shrill affright!
Untaught, yet wise! mid all thy brief alarms
Thou closely clingest to thy Mother's arms,
Nestling thy little face in that fond breast
Whose anxious heavings lull thee to thy rest!
Man's breathing Miniature! thou mak'st me sigh –
A Babe art thou – and such a Thing am I!
To anger rapid and as soon appeased,
For trifles mourning and by trifles pleased,
Break Friendship's mirror with a tetchy blow,
Yet snatch what coals of fire on Pleasure's altar glow!

O thou that rearest with celestial aim
The future Seraph in my mortal frame,
Thrice holy Faith! whatever thorns I meet
As on I totter with unpractised feet,
Still let me stretch my arms and cling to thee,
Meek nurse of souls through their long infancy!
1795

TO THE REV. GEORGE COLERIDGE

Of Ottery St Mary, Devon

A blessed lot hath he, who having passed
His youth and early manhood in the stir
And turmoil of the world, retreats at length,
With cares that move, not agitate the heart,
To the same dwelling where his father dwelt;
And haply views his tottering little ones
Embrace those aged knees and climb that lap,
On which first kneeling his own infancy
Lisped its brief prayer. Such, O my earliest Friend!
Thy lot, and such thy brothers too enjoy.
At distance did ye climb life's upland road,
Yet cheered and cheering: now fraternal love
Hath drawn you to one centre. Be your days
Holy, and blest and blessing may ye live!

To me the Eternal Wisdom hath dispensed
A different fortune and more different mind –
Me from the spot where first I sprang to light
Too soon transplanted, ere my soul had fixed
Its first domestic loves; and hence through life
Chasing chance-started friendships. A brief while
Some have preserved me from life's pelting ills;
But, like a tree with leaves of feeble stem,
If the clouds lasted, and a sudden breeze
Ruffled the boughs, they on my head at once
Dropped the collected shower; and some most false,
False and fair foliaged as the Manchineel,
Have tempted me to slumber in their shade
E'en mid the storm; then breathing subtlest damps,
Mixed their own venom with the rain from Heaven,
That I woke poisoned! But, all praise to Him

Who gives us all things, more have yielded me
Permanent shelter; and beside one friend,
Beneath the impervious covert of one oak,
I've raised a lowly shed, and know the names
Of husband and of father; not unhearing
Of that divine and nightly-whispering voice,
Which from my childhood to maturer years
Spake to me of predestinated wreaths,
Bright with no fading colours! Yet at times
My soul is sad, that I have roamed through life
Still most a stranger, most with naked heart
At mine own home and birth-place: chiefly then,
When I remember thee, my earliest friend!
Thee, who didst watch my boyhood and my youth;
Didst trace my wanderings with a father's eye;
And boding evil yet still hoping good,
Rebuk'd each fault, and over all my woes
Sorrowed in silence! He who counts alone
The beatings of the solitary heart,
That being knows, how I have loved thee ever,
Loved as a brother, as a son revered thee!
Oh! 'tis to me an ever new delight,
To talk of thee and thine: or when the blast
Of the shrill winter, rattling our rude sash,
Endears the cleanly hearth and social bowl;
Or when as now, on some delicious eve,
We in our sweet sequestered orchard plot
Sit on the tree crooked earth-ward; whose old boughs,
That hang above us in an arborous roof,
Stirred by the faint gale of departing May,
Send their loose blossoms slanting o'er our heads!

Nor dost not thou sometimes recall those hours,
When with the joy of hope thou gav'st thine ear
To my wild firstling-lays. Since then my song

Hath sounded deeper notes, such as beseem
Or that sad wisdom folly leaves behind,
Or such as, tuned to these tumultuous times,
Cope with the tempest's swell! These various strains,
Which I have framed in many a various mood,
Accept, my brother! and (for some perchance
Will strike discordant on thy milder mind)
If aught of error or intemperate truth
Should meet thine ear, think thou that riper age
Will calm it down, and let thy love forgive it!
1797

THIS LIME-TREE BOWER MY PRISON

Addressed to Charles Lamb, of the India House, London

In the June of 1797 some long-expected friends paid a visit to the author's cottage; and on the morning of their arrival, he met with an accident, which disabled him from walking during the whole time of their stay. One evening, when they had left him for a few hours, he composed the following lines in the garden-bower.

Well, they are gone, and here I must remain,
This lime-tree bower my prison! I have lost
Beauties and feelings, such as would have been
Most sweet to my remembrance even when age
Had dimmed mine eyes to blindness! They, meanwhile,
Friends, whom I never more may meet again,
On springy heath, along the hill-top edge,
Wander in gladness, and wind down, perchance,
To that still roaring dell, of which I told;
The roaring dell, o'erwooded, narrow, deep,
And only speckled by the midday sun;
Where its slim trunk the ash from rock to rock
Flings arching like a bridge; – that branchless ash,
Unsunned and damp, whose few poor yellow leaves
Ne'er tremble in the gale, yet tremble still,
Fanned by the water-fall! and there my friends
Behold the dark green file of long lank weeds,
That all at once (a most fantastic sight!)
Still nod and drip beneath the dripping edge
Of the blue clay-stone.

                              Now, my friends emerge
Beneath the wide wide Heaven – and view again
The many-steepled tract magnificent
Of hilly fields and meadows, and the sea,

With some fair bark, perhaps, whose sails light up
The slip of smooth clear blue betwixt two isles
Of purple shadow! Yes! they wander on
In gladness all; but thou, methinks, most glad,
My gentle-hearted Charles! for thou hast pined
And hungered after Nature, many a year,
In the great city pent, winning thy way
With sad yet patient soul, through evil and pain
And strange calamity! Ah! slowly sink
Behind the western ridge, thou glorious sun!
Shine in the slant beams of the sinking orb,
Ye purple heath-flowers! richlier burn, ye clouds!
Live in the yellow light, ye distant groves!
And kindle, thou blue ocean! So my Friend
Struck with deep joy may stand, as I have stood,
Silent with swimming sense; yea, gazing round
On the wide landscape, gaze till all doth seem
Less gross than bodily; and of such hues
As veil the Almighty Spirit, when yet he makes
Spirits perceive his presence.

                A delight
Comes sudden to my heart, and I am glad
As I myself were there! Nor in this bower,
This little lime-tree bower, have I not marked
Much that has soothed me. Pale beneath the blaze
Hung the transparent foliage; and I watch'd
Some broad and sunny leaf, and loved to see
The shadow of the leaf and stem above
Dappling its sunshine! And that walnut-tree
Was richly tinged, and a deep radiance lay
Full on the ancient ivy, which usurps
Those fronting elms, and now, with blackest mass
Makes their dark branches gleam a lighter hue
Through the late twilight: and though now the bat

Wheels silent by, and not a swallow twitters,
Yet still the solitary humble bee
Sings in the bean-flower! Henceforth I shall know
That Nature ne'er deserts the wise and pure;
No plot so narrow, be but Nature there,
No waste so vacant, but may well employ
Each faculty of sense, and keep the heart
Awake to Love and Beauty! and sometimes
'Tis well to be bereft of promised good,
That we may lift the Soul, and contemplate
With lively joy the joys we cannot share.
My gentle-hearted Charles! when the last rook
Beat its straight path along the dusky air
Homewards, I blest it! deeming its black wing
(Now a dim speck, now vanishing in light)
Had cross'd the mighty orb's dilated glory,
While thou stood'st gazing; or when all was still,
Flew creeking o'er thy head, and had a charm
For thee, my gentle-hearted Charles, to whom
No sound is dissonant which tells of Life.
1797

THE RIME OF THE ANCIENT MARINER

Part I

It is an ancient Mariner,
And he stoppeth one of three.
'By thy long grey beard and glittering eye,
Now wherefore stopp'st thou me?

'The Bridegroom's doors are opened wide,
And I am next of kin;
The guests are met, the feast is set:
May'st hear the merry din.'

He holds him with his skinny hand,
'There was a ship,' quoth he.
'Hold off! unhand me, grey-beard loon!'
Eftsoons his hand dropt he.

He holds him with his glittering eye –
The Wedding Guest stood still,
And listens like a three years' child:
The Mariner hath his will.

The Wedding Guest sat on a stone:
He cannot choose but hear;
And thus spake on that ancient man,
The bright-eyed Mariner.

'The ship was cheered, the harbour cleared,
Merrily did we drop
Below the kirk, below the hill,
Below the lighthouse top.

'The sun came up upon the left,
Out of the sea came he!

And he shone bright, and on the right
Went down into the sea.

'Higher and higher every day,
Till over the mast at noon –'
The Wedding Guest here beat his breast,
For he heard the loud bassoon.

The Bride hath paced into the hall,
Red as a rose is she;
Nodding their heads before her goes
The merry minstrelsy.

The Wedding Guest he beat his breast,
Yet he cannot choose but hear;
And thus spake on that ancient man,
The bright-eyed Mariner.

And now the storm-blast came, and he
Was tyrannous and strong:
He struck with his o'ertaking wings,
And chased us south along.

With sloping masts and dipping prow,
As who pursued with yell and blow
Still treads the shadow of his foe,
And forward bends his head,
The ship drove fast, loud roared the blast,
And southward aye we fled.

And now there came both mist and snow,
And it grew wondrous cold:
And ice, mast-high, came floating by,
As green as emerald.

And through the drifts the snowy cliffs
Did send a dismal sheen:
Nor shapes of men nor beasts we ken –
The ice was all between.

The ice was here, the ice was there,
The ice was all around:
It cracked and growled, and roared and howled,
Like noises in a swound!

At length did cross an Albatross,
Through the fog it came;
As if it had been a Christian soul,
We hailed it in God's name.

It ate the food it ne'er had eat,
And round and round it flew.
The ice did split with a thunder-fit;
The helmsman steered us through!

And a good south wind sprung up behind;
The Albatross did follow,
And every day, for food or play,
Came to the mariner's hollo!

In mist or cloud, on mast or shroud,
It perched for vespers nine;
Whiles all the night, through fog-smoke white,
Glimmered the white moonshine.

'God save thee, ancient Mariner!
From the fiends, that plague thee thus! –
Why look'st thou so?' – With my crossbow
I shot the Albatross.

Part II

The Sun now rose upon the right:
Out of the sea came he,
Still hid in mist, and on the left
Went down into the sea.

And the good south wind still blew behind,
But no sweet bird did follow,
Nor any day for food or play
Came to the mariners' hollo!

And I had done a hellish thing,
And it would work 'em woe:
For all averred, I had killed the bird
That made the breeze to blow.
Ah wretch! said they, the bird to slay,
That made the breeze to blow!

Nor dim nor red, like God's own head,
The glorious Sun uprist:
Then all averred, I had killed the bird
That brought the fog and mist.
'Twas right, said they, such birds to slay,
That bring the fog and mist.

The fair breeze blew, the white foam flew,
The furrow followed free;
We were the first that ever burst
Into that silent sea.

Down dropt the breeze, the sails dropt down,
'Twas sad as sad could be;
And we did speak only to break
The silence of the sea!

All in a hot and copper sky,
The bloody Sun, at noon,
Right up above the mast did stand,
No bigger than the Moon.

Day after day, day after day,
We stuck, nor breath nor motion;
As idle as a painted ship
Upon a painted ocean.

Water, water, every-where,
And all the boards did shrink;
Water, water, every-where,
Nor any drop to drink.

The very deep did rot: O Christ!
That ever this should be!
Yea, slimy things did crawl with legs
Upon the slimy sea.

About, about, in reel and rout
The death-fires danced at night;
The water, like a witch's oils,
Burnt green, and blue and white.

And some in dreams assured were
Of the spirit that plagues us so;
Nine fathom deep he had followed us
From the land of mist and snow.

And every tongue, through utter drought,
Was withered at the root;
We could not speak, no more than if
We had been choked with soot.

Ah! well a-day! what evil looks
Had I from old and young!
Instead of the cross, the Albatross
About my neck was hung.

Part III

There passed a weary time. Each throat
Was parched, and glazed each eye.
A weary time! a weary time!
How glazed each weary eye,
When looking westward, I beheld
A something in the sky.

At first it seemed a little speck,
And then it seemed a mist;
It moved and moved, and took at last
A certain shape, I wist.

A speck, a mist, a shape, I wist!
And still it neared and neared:
As if it dodged a water-sprite,
It plunged and tacked and veered.

With throats unslaked, with black lips baked,
We could nor laugh nor wail;
Through utter drought all dumb we stood!
I bit my arm, I sucked the blood,
And cried, A sail! a sail!

With throats unslaked, with black lips baked,
Agape they heard me call:
Gramercy! they for joy did grin,
And all at once their breath drew in,
As they were drinking all.

See! see! (I cried) she tacks no more!
Hither to work us weal;
Without a breeze, without a tide,
She steadies with upright keel!

The western wave was all aflame.
The day was well nigh done!
Almost upon the western wave
Rested the broad bright Sun;
When that strange shape drove suddenly
Betwixt us and the Sun.

And straight the Sun was flecked with bars
(Heaven's Mother and send us grace!),
As if through a dungeon-grate he peered
With broad and burning face.

Alas! (thought I, and my heart beat loud)
How fast she nears and nears!
Are those her sails that glance in the Sun,
Like restless gossameres?

Are those her ribs through which the Sun
Did peer, as through a grate?
And is that Woman all her crew?
Is that a Death? and are there two?
Is Death that woman's mate?

Her lips were red, her looks were free,
Her locks were yellow as gold:
Her skin was as white as leprosy,
The Nightmare Life-in-Death was she,
Who thicks man's blood with cold.

The naked hulk alongside came,
And the twain were casting dice;
'The game is done! I've won! I've won!'
Quoth she, and whistles thrice.

The Sun's rim dips; the stars rush out:
At one stride comes the dark;
With far-heard whisper, o'er the sea,
Off shot the spectre bark.

We listened and looked sideways up!
Fear at my heart, as at a cup,
My life-blood seemed to sip!
The stars were dim, and thick the night,
The steersman's face by his lamp gleamed white;
From the sails the dew did drip –
Till clomb above the eastern bar
The horned Moon, with one bright star
Within the nether tip.

One after one, by the star-dogged Moon,
Too quick for groan or sigh,
Each turned his face with a ghastly pang,
And cursed me with his eye.

Four times fifty living men
(And I heard nor sigh nor groan),
With heavy thump, a lifeless lump,
They dropped down one by one.

The souls did from their bodies fly –
They fled to bliss or woe!
And every soul, it passed me by,
Like the whizz of my crossbow!

Part IV

'I fear thee, ancient Mariner!
I fear thy skinny hand!
And thou art long, and lank, and brown,
As is the ribbed sea-sand.

'I fear thee and thy glittering eye,
And thy skinny hand, so brown.' –
Fear not, fear not, thou Wedding Guest!
This body dropt not down.

Alone, alone, all, all alone,
Alone on a wide, wide sea!
And never a saint took pity on
My soul in agony.

The many men, so beautiful!
And they all dead did lie:
And a thousand thousand slimy things
Lived on; and so did I.

I looked upon the rotting sea,
And drew my eyes away;
I looked upon the rotting deck,
And there the dead men lay.

I looked to Heaven, and tried to pray;
But or ever a prayer had gushed,
A wicked whisper came, and made
My heart as dry as dust.

I closed my lids, and kept them close,
And the balls like pulses beat;
For the sky and the sea, and the sea and the sky
Lay like a load on my weary eye,
And the dead were at my feet.

The cold sweat melted from their limbs,
Nor rot nor reek did they:
The look with which they looked on me
Had never passed away.

An orphan's curse would drag to hell
A spirit from on high;
But oh! more horrible than that
Is the curse in a dead man's eye!
Seven days, seven nights, I saw that curse,
And yet I could not die.

The moving Moon went up the sky.
And nowhere did abide:
Softly she was going up,
And a star or two beside –

Her beams bemocked the sultry main,
Like April hoar-frost spread;
But where the ship's huge shadow lay,
The charmed water burnt alway
A still and awful red.

Beyond the shadow of the ship,
I watched the water-snakes:
They moved in tracks of shining white,
And when they reared, the elfish light
Fell off in hoary flakes.

Within the shadow of the ship
I watched their rich attire:
Blue, glossy green, and velvet black,
They coiled and swam; and every track
Was a flash of golden fire.

O happy living things! no tongue
Their beauty might declare:
A spring of love gushed from my heart,
And I blessed them unaware:
Sure my kind saint took pity on me,
And I blessed them unaware.

The self-same moment I could pray;
And from my neck so free
The Albatross fell off, and sank
Like lead into the sea.

Part V

Oh sleep! it is a gentle thing,
Beloved from pole to pole!
To Mary Queen the praise be given!
She sent the gentle sleep from Heaven,
That slid into my soul.

The silly buckets on the deck,
That had so long remained,
I dreamt that they were filled with dew;
And when I awoke, it rained.

My lips were wet, my throat was cold,
My garments all were dank;
Sure I had drunken in my dreams,
And still my body drank.

I moved, and could not feel my limbs:
I was so light – almost
I thought that I had died in sleep,
And was a blessed ghost.

And soon I heard a roaring wind:
It did not come anear;
But with its sound it shook the sails,
That were so thin and sere.

The upper air burst into life!
And a hundred fire-flags sheen,
To and fro they were hurried about!
And to and fro, and in and out,
The wan stars danced between.

And the coming wind did roar more loud,
And the sails did sigh like sedge;
And the rain poured down from one black cloud;
The Moon was at its edge.

The thick black cloud was cleft, and still
The Moon was at its side:
Like waters shot from some high crag,
The lightning fell with never a jag,
A river steep and wide.

The loud wind never reached the ship,
Yet now the ship moved on!
Beneath the lightning and the Moon
The dead men gave a groan.

They groaned, they stirred, they all uprose,
Nor spake, nor moved their eyes;
It had been strange, even in a dream,
To have seen those dead men rise.

The helmsman steered, the ship moved on;
Yet never a breeze up blew;
The mariners all 'gan work the ropes,
Where they were wont to do;
They raised their limbs like lifeless tools —
We were a ghastly crew.

The body of my brother's son
Stood by me, knee to knee:
The body and I pulled at one rope,
But he said nought to me.

'I fear thee, ancient Mariner!'
Be calm, thou Wedding Guest!
'Twas not those souls that fled in pain,
Which to their corses came again,
But a troop of spirits blest:

For when it dawned — they dropped their arms,
And clustered round the mast;
Sweet sounds rose slowly through their mouths,
And from their bodies passed.

Around, around, flew each sweet sound,
Then darted to the Sun;
Slowly the sounds came back again,
Now mixed, now one by one.

Sometimes a-dropping from the sky
I heard the sky-lark sing;
Sometimes all little birds that are,
How they seemed to fill the sea and air
With their sweet jargoning!

And now 'twas like all instruments,
Now like a lonely flute;
And now it is an angel's song,
That makes the heavens be mute.

It ceased; yet still the sails made on
A pleasant noise till noon,
A noise like of a hidden brook
In the leafy month of June,
That to the sleeping woods all night
Singeth a quiet tune.

Till noon we quietly sailed on,
Yet never a breeze did breathe:
Slowly and smoothly went the ship,
Moved onward from beneath.

Under the keel nine fathom deep,
From the land of mist and snow,
The spirit slid: and it was he
That made the ship to go.
The sails at noon left off their tune,
And the ship stood still also.

The Sun, right up above the mast,
Had fixed her to the ocean:
But in a minute she 'gan stir,
With a short uneasy motion –
Backwards and forwards half her length
With a short uneasy motion.

Then like a pawing horse let go,
She made a sudden bound:
If flung the blood into my head,
And I fell down in a swound.

How long in that same fit I lay,
I have not to declare;
But ere my living life returned,
I heard, and in my soul discerned
Two voices in the air.

'Is it he?' quoth one. 'Is this the man?
By him who died on cross,
With his cruel bow he laid full low
The harmless Albatross.

'The spirit who bideth by himself
In the land of mist and snow,
He loved the bird that loved the man
Who shot him with his bow.'

The other was a softer voice,
As soft as honey-dew:
Quoth he, 'The man hath penance done,
And penance more will do.'

Part VI

First Voice

But tell me, tell me! speak again,
Thy soft response renewing –
What makes that ship drive on so fast?
What is the ocean doing?

Second Voice

Still as a slave before his lord,
The ocean hath no blast;
His great bright eye most silently
Up to the Moon is cast –

If he may know which way to go;
For she guides him smooth or grim.
See, brother, see! how graciously
She looketh down on him.

First Voice

But why drives on that ship so fast,
Without or wave or wind?

Second Voice

The air is cut away before,
And closes from behind.

Fly, brother, fly! more high, more high!
Or we shall be belated:
For slow and slow that ship will go,
When the Mariner's trance is abated.

I woke, and we were sailing on
As in a gentle weather:
'Twas night, calm night, the Moon was high;
The dead men stood together.

All stood together on the deck,
For a charnel-dungeon fitter:
All fixed on me their stony eyes,
That in the Moon did glitter.

The pang, the curse, with which they died,
Had never passed away:
I could not draw my eyes from theirs,
Nor turn them up to pray.

And now this spell was snapt: once more
I viewed the ocean green,
And looked far forth, yet little saw
Of what had else been seen –

Like one, that on a lonesome road
Doth walk in fear and dread,
And having once turned round walks on,
And turns no more his head;
Because he knows, a frightful fiend
Doth close behind him tread.

But soon there breathed a wind on me,
Nor sound nor motion made:
Its path was not upon the sea,
In ripple or in shade.

It raised my hair, it fanned my cheek
Like a meadow-gale of Spring –
It mingled strangely with my fears,
Yet it felt like a welcoming.

Swiftly, swiftly flew the ship,
Yet she sailed softly too:
Sweetly, sweetly blew the breeze –
On me alone it blew.

Oh! dream of joy! is this indeed
The lighthouse top I see?
Is this the hill? is this the kirk?
Is this mine own countree?

We drifted o'er the harbour-bay,
And I with sobs did pray –
O let me be awake, my God!
Or let me sleep alway.

The harbour-bay was clear as glass,
So smoothly it was strewn!
And on the bay the moonlight lay,
And the shadow of the Moon.

The rock shone bright, the kirk no less,
That stands above the rock:
The moonlight steeped in silentness
The steady weathercock.

And the bay was white with silent light,
Till rising from the same,
Full many shapes, that shadows were,
In crimson colours came.

A little distance from the prow
Those crimson shadows were:
I turned my eyes upon the deck –
Oh, Christ! what saw I there!

Each corse lay flat, lifeless and flat,
And, by the holy rood!
A man all light, a seraph-man,
On every corse there stood.

This seraph-band, each waved his hand:
It was a heavenly sight!
They stood as signals to the land,
Each one a lovely light;

This seraph-band, each waved his hand,
No voice did they impart –
No voice; but oh! the silence sank
Like music on my heart.

But soon I heard the dash of oars,
I heard the Pilot's cheer;
My head was turned perforce away,
And I saw a boat appear.

The Pilot and the Pilot's boy,
I heard them coming fast:
Dear Lord in Heaven! it was a joy
The dead men could not blast.

I saw a third – I heard his voice:
It is the Hermit good!
He singeth loud his godly hymns
That he makes in the wood.
He'll shrieve my soul, he'll wash away
The Albatross's blood.

Part VII

This Hermit good lives in that wood
Which slopes down to the sea.
How loudly his sweet voice he rears!
He loves to talk with marineres
That come from a far countree.

He kneels at morn, and noon, and eve –
He hath a cushion plump:
It is the moss that wholly hides
The rotted old oak stump.

The skiff-boat neared: I heard them talk,
'Why, this is strange, I trow!
Where are those lights so many and fair,
That signal made but now?'

'Strange, by my faith!' the Hermit said –
'And they answered not our cheer!
The planks looked warped! and see those sails,
How thin they are and sere!
I never saw aught like to them,
Unless perchance it were

'Brown skeletons of leaves that lag
My forest brook along;
When the ivy-tod is heavy with snow,
And the owlet whoops to the wolf below,
That eats the she-wolf's young.'

'Dear Lord! it hath a fiendish look –
(The Pilot made reply)
I am afeared – 'Push on, push on!'
Said the Hermit cheerily.

The boat came closer to the ship,
But I nor spake nor stirred;
The boat came close beneath the ship,
And straight a sound was heard.

Under the water it rumbled on,
Still louder and more dread:
It reached the ship, it split the bay;
The ship went down like lead.

Stunned by that loud and dreadful sound,
Which sky and ocean smote,
Like one that hath been seven days drowned
My body lay afloat;
But swift as dreams, myself I found
Within the Pilot's boat.

Upon the whirl, where sank the ship,
The board spun round and round;
And all was still, save that the hill
Was telling of the sound.

I moved my lips – the Pilot shrieked
And fell down in a fit;

The holy Hermit raised his eyes,
And prayed where he did sit.

I took the oars: the Pilot's boy,
Who now doth crazy go,
Laughed loud and long, and all the while
His eyes went to and fro.
'Ha! ha!' quoth he, 'full plain I see,
The Devil knows how to row.'

And now, all in my own countree,
I stood on the firm land!
The Hermit stepped forth from the boat,
And scarcely he could stand.

'O shrieve me, shrieve me, holy man!'
The Hermit crossed his brow.
'Say quick,' quoth he, 'I bid thee say –
What manner of man art thou?'

Forthwith this frame of mine was wrenched
With a woeful agony,
Which forced me to begin my tale;
And then it left me free.

Since then, at an uncertain hour,
That agony returns:
And till my ghastly tale is told,
This heart within me burns.

I pass, like night, from land to land;
I have strange power of speech;
That moment that his face I see,
I know the man that must hear me:
To him my tale I teach.

What loud uproar bursts from that door!
The wedding guests are there:
But in the garden bower the Bride
And bride-maids singing are:
And hark the little vesper bell,
Which biddeth me to prayer!

O Wedding Guest! this soul hath been
Alone on a wide, wide sea:
So lonely 'twas, that God himself
Scarce seemed there to be.

O sweeter than the marriage feast,
'Tis sweeter far to me,
To walk together to the kirk
With a goodly company! –

To walk together to the kirk,
And all together pray,
While each to his great Father bends,
Old men, and babes, and loving friends
And youths and maidens gay!

Farewell, farewell! but this I tell
To thee, thou Wedding Guest!
He prayeth well, who loveth well
Both man and bird and beast.

He prayeth best, who loveth best
All things both great and small;
For the dear God who loveth us,
He made and loveth all.

The Mariner, whose eye is bright,
Whose beard with age is hoar,

Is gone: and now the Wedding Guest
Turned from the Bridegroom's door.

He went like one that hath been stunned,
And is of sense forlorn:
A sadder and a wiser man,
He rose the morrow morn.
1798

FEARS IN SOLITUDE

Written in April 1798, during the alarm of an invasion

A green and silent spot, amid the hills,
A small and silent dell! O'er stiller place
No singing sky-lark ever poised himself.
The hills are heathy, save that swelling slope,
Which hath a gay and gorgeous covering on,
All golden with the never-bloomless furze,
Which now blooms most profusely: but the dell,
Bathed by the mist, is fresh and delicate
As vernal cornfield, or the unripe flax,
When, through its half-transparent stalks, at eve,
The level sunshine glimmers with green light.
Oh! 'tis a quiet spirit-healing nook!
Which all, methinks, would love; but chiefly he,
The humble man, who, in his youthful years,
Knew just so much of folly, as had made
His early manhood more securely wise!
Here he might lie on fern or withered heath,
While from the singing-lark (that sings unseen
The minstrelsy that solitude loves best),
And from the sun, and from the breezy air,
Sweet influences trembled o'er his frame;
And he, with many feelings, many thoughts,
Made up a meditative joy, and found
Religious meanings in the forms of Nature!
And so, his sense gradually wrapt
In a half sleep, he dreams of better worlds,
And dreaming hears thee still, O singing-lark;
That singest like an angel in the clouds!

My God! it is a melancholy thing
For such a man, who would full fain preserve
His soul in calmness, yet perforce must feel
For all his human brethren – O my God!
It weighs upon the heart, that he must think
What uproar and what strife may now be stirring
This way or that way o'er these silent hills –
Invasion, and the thunder and the shout,
And all the crash of onset; fear and rage,
And undetermined conflict – even now,
Even now, perchance, and in his native isle:
Carnage and groans beneath this blessed sun!
We have offended, O my countrymen!
We have offended very grievously,
And been most tyrannous. From east to west
A groan of accusation pierces Heaven!
The wretched plead against us; multitudes
Countless and vehement, the sons of God,
Our brethren! Like a cloud that travels on,
Steamed up from Cairo's swamps of pestilence,
Even so, my countrymen! have we gone forth
And borne to distant tribes slavery and pangs,
And, deadlier far, our vices, whose deep taint
With slow perdition murders the whole man,
His body and his soul! Meanwhile, at home,
All individual dignity and power
Engulfed in courts, committees, institutions,
Associations and societies,
A vain, speech-mouthing, speech-reporting guild,
One benefit club for mutual flattery.
We have drunk up, demure as at a grace,
Pollutions from the brimming cup of wealth;
Contemptuous of all honourable rule,
Yet bartering freedom and the poor man's life
For gold, as at a market! The sweet words

Of Christian promise, words that even yet
Might stem destruction, were they wisely preached,
Are muttered o'er by men, whose tones proclaim
How flat and wearisome they feel their trade:
Rank scoffers some, but most too indolent
To deem them falsehoods or to know their truth.
Oh! blasphemous! the book of life is made
A superstitious instrument, on which
We gabble o'er the oaths we mean to break;
For all must swear – all and in every place,
College and wharf, council and justice court;
All, all must swear, the briber and the bribed,
Merchant and lawyer, senator and priest,
The rich, the poor, the old man and the young;
All, all make up one scheme of perjury,
That faith doth reel; the very name of God
Sounds like a juggler's charm; and, bold with joy,
Forth from his dark and lonely hiding place,
(Portentious sight!) the owlet Atheism,
Sailing on obscene wings athwart the noon,
Drops his blue-fringed lids, and holds them close,
And hooting at the glorious sun in Heaven,
Cries out, 'Where is it?'

                              Thankless too for peace
(Peace long preserved by fleets and perilous seas),
Secure from actual warfare, we have loved
To swell the war-whoop, passionate for war!
Alas! for ages ignorant of all
Its ghastlier workings (famine or blue plague,
Battle, or siege, or flight through wintry snows),
We, this whole people, have been clamorous
For war and bloodshed; animating sports,
The which we pay for as a thing to talk of,
Spectators and not combatants! No guess

Anticipative of a wrong unfelt,
No speculation on contingency,
However dim and vague, too vague and dim
To yield a justifying cause; and forth
(Stuffed out with big preamble, holy names,
And adjurations of the God in Heaven),
We send out mandates for the certain death
Of thousands and ten thousands! Boys and girls,
And women, that would groan to see a child
Pull off an insect's leg, all read of war,
The best amusement for our morning meal!
The poor wretch, who has learnt his only prayers
From curses, who knows scarcely words enough
To ask a blessing from his Heavenly Father,
Becomes a fluent phraseman, absolute
And technical in victories and defeats,
And all our dainty terms for fratricide;
Terms which we trundle smoothly o'er our tongues
Like mere abstractions, empty sounds to which
We join no feeling and attach no form!
As if the soldier died without a wound;
As if the fibres of this godlike frame
Were gored without a pang; as if the wretch
Who fell in battle, doing bloody deeds,
Passed off to Heaven, translated and not killed;
As though he had no wife to pine for him,
No God to judge him! Therefore, evil days
Are coming on us, O my countrymen!
And what if all-avenging Providence,
Strong and retributive, should make us know
The meaning of our words, force us to feel
The desolation and the agony
Of our fierce doings!

                         Spare us yet awhile,
Father and God! O spare us yet awhile!
Oh! let not English women drag their flight
Fainting beneath the burthen of their babes,
Of the sweet infants, that but yesterday
Laughed at the breast! Sons, brothers, husbands, all
Who ever gazed with fondness on the forms
Which grew up with you round the same fireside,
And all who ever heard the sabbath bells
Without the infidel's scorn, make yourselves pure!
Stand forth! be men! repel an impious foe,
Impious and false, a light yet cruel race,
Who laugh away all virtue, mingling mirth
With deeds of murder; and still promising
Freedom, themselves too sensual to be free,
Poison life's amities, and cheat the heart
Of faith and quiet hope, and all that soothes
And all that lifts the spirit! Stand we forth;
Render them back upon the insulted ocean,
And let them toss as idly on its waves
As the vile seaweed, which some mountain blast
Swept from our shores! And oh! may we return
Not with a drunken triumph, but with fear,
Repenting of the wrongs with which we stung
So fierce a foe to frenzy!

                         I have told,
O Britons! O my brethren! I have told
Most bitter truth, but without bitterness.
Nor deem my zeal or factious or mistimed;
For never can true courage dwell with them,
Who, playing tricks with conscience, dare not look
At their own vices. We have been too long
Dupes of a deep delusion! Some, belike,
Groaning with restless enmity, expect

All change from change of constituted power;
As if a government had been a robe,
On which our vice and wretchedness were tagged
Like fancy-points and fringes, with the robe
Pulled off at pleasure. Fondly these attach
A radical causation to a few
Poor drudges of chastising Providence,
Who borrow all their hues and qualities
From our own folly and rank wickedness,
Which gave them birth and nursed them. Others, meanwhile,
Dote with a mad idolatry; and all
Who will not fall before their images,
And yield them worship, they are enemies
Even of their country!

           Such have I been deemed –
But, O dear Britain! O my Mother Isle!
Needs must thou prove a name most dear and holy
To me, a son, a brother, and a friend,
A husband, and a father! who revere
All bonds of natural love, and find them all
Within the limits of thy rocky shores.
O native Britain! O my Mother Isle!
How shouldst thou prove aught else but dear and holy
To me, who from thy lakes and mountain-hills,
Thy clouds, thy quiet dales, thy rocks and seas,
Have drunk in all my intellectual life,
All sweet sensations, all ennobling thoughts,
All adoration of the God in nature,
All lovely and all honourable things,
Whatever makes this mortal spirit feel
The joy and greatness of its future being?
There lives nor form nor feeling on my soul
Unborrowed from my country. O divine
And beauteous island! thou hast been my sole

And most magnificent temple, in the which
I walk with awe, and sing my stately songs,
Loving the God that made me!

               May my fears,
My filial fears, be vain! and may the vaunts
And menace of the vengeful enemy
Pass like the gust, that roared and died away
In the distant tree: which heard, and only heard
In this low dell, bowed not the delicate grass.

  But now the gentle dew-fall sends abroad
The fruit-like perfume of the golden furze:
The light has left the summit of the hill,
Though still a sunny gleam lies beautiful,
Aslant the ivied beacon. Now farewell,
Farewell, awhile, O soft and silent spot!
On the green sheep-track, up the heathy hill,
Homeward I wind my way; and lo! recalled
From bodings that have well nigh wearied me,
I find myself upon the brow, and pause
Startled! And after lonely sojourning
In such a quiet and surrounded nook,
This burst of prospect, here the shadowy main,
Dim tinted, there the mighty majesty
Of that huge amphitheatre of rich
And elmy fields, seems like society –
Conversing with the mind, and giving it
A livelier impulse and a dance of thought!
And now, beloved Stowey! I behold
Thy church tower, and, methinks, the four huge elms
Clustering, which mark the mansion of my friend;
And close behind them, hidden from my view,
Is my own lowly cottage, where my babe
And my babe's mother dwell in peace! With light

And quickened footsteps thitherward I tend,
Remembering thee, O green and silent dell!
And grateful, that by Nature's quietness
And solitary musings, all my heart
Is softened, and made worthy to indulge
Love, and the thoughts that yearn for human kind.
1798

FROST AT MIDNIGHT

The frost performs its secret ministry,
Unhelped by any wind. The owlet's cry
Came loud – and hark, again! loud as before.
The inmates of my cottage, all at rest,
Have left me to that solitude, which suits
Abstruser musings: save that at my side
My cradled infant slumbers peacefully.
'Tis calm indeed! so calm, that it disturbs
And vexes meditation with its strange
And extreme silentness. Sea, hill, and wood,
This populous village! Sea, and hill, and wood,
With the numberless goings-on of life,
Inaudible as dreams! the thin blue flame
Lies on my low burnt fire, and quivers not;
Only that film, which fluttered on the grate,
Still flutters there, the sole unquiet thing.
Methinks, its motion in this hush of nature
Gives it dim sympathies with me who live,
Making it a companionable form,
Whose puny flaps and freaks the idling Spirit
By its own moods interprets, everywhere
Echo or mirror seeking of itself,
And makes a toy of Thought.

                                    But O! how oft,
How oft, at school, with most believing mind,
Presageful, have I gazed upon the bars,
To watch that fluttering stranger! and as oft
With unclosed lids, already had I dreamt
Of my sweet birthplace, and the old church tower,
Whose bells, the poor man's only music, rang
From morn to evening, all the hot Fair-day,
So sweetly, that they stirred and haunted me

With a wild pleasure, falling on mine ear
Most like articulate sounds of things to come!
So gazed I, till the soothing things I dreamt
Lulled me to sleep, and sleep prolonged my dreams!
And so I brooded all the following morn,
Awed by the stern preceptor's face, mine eye
Fixed with mock study on my swimming book:
Save if the door half opened, and I snatched
A hasty glance, and still my heart leaped up,
For still I hoped to see the *stranger's* face,
Townsman, or aunt, or sister more beloved,
My play-mate when we both were clothed alike!

    Dear Babe, that sleepest cradled by my side,
Whose gentle breathings, heard in this deep calm,
Fill up the interspersed vacancies
And momentary pauses of the thought!
My babe so beautiful! it thrills my heart
With tender gladness, thus to look at thee,
And think that thou shalt learn far other lore
And in far other scenes! For I was reared
In the great city, pent 'mid cloisters dim,
And saw nought lovely but the sky and stars.
But thou, my babe! shalt wander like a breeze
By lakes and sandy shores, beneath the crags
Of ancient mountain, and beneath the clouds,
Which image in their bulk both lakes and shores
And mountain crags: so shalt thou see and hear
The lovely shapes and sounds intelligible
Of that eternal language, which thy God
Utters, who from eternity doth teach
Himself in all, and all things in himself.
Great universal Teacher! he shall mould
Thy spirit, and by giving make it ask.

Therefore all seasons shall be sweet to thee,
Whether the summer clothe the general earth
With greenness, or the redbreast sit and sing
Betwixt the tufts of snow on the bare branch
Of mossy apple tree, while the nigh thatch
Smokes in the sun-thaw; whether the eave-drops fall
Heard only in the trances of the blast,
Or if the secret ministry of frost
Shall hang them up in silent icicles,
Quietly shining to the quiet Moon.
1798

LINES

Written in the Album in Elbingerode,
in the Hartz Forest

I stood on Brocken's sovran height, and saw
Woods crowding upon woods, hills over hills,
A surging scene, and only limited
By the blue distance. Heavily my way
Downward I dragged through fir groves evermore,
Where bright green moss heaves in sepulchral forms
Speckled with sunshine; and, but seldom heard,
The sweet bird's song became a hollow sound;
And the breeze, murmuring indivisibly,
Preserved its solemn murmur most distinct
From many a note of many a waterfall,
And the brook's chatter; 'mid whose islet stones
The dingy kidling with its tinkling bell
Leaped frolicsome, or old romantic goat
Sat, his white beard slow waving. I moved on
In low and languid mood: for I had found
That outward forms, the loftiest, still receive
Their finer influence from the Life within –
Fair cyphers else: fair, but of import vague
Or unconcerning, where the heart not finds
History or prophecy of friend, or child,
Or gentle maid, our first and early love,
Or father, or the venerable name
Of our adored country! O thou Queen,
Thou delegated Deity of Earth,
O dear, dear England! how my longing eye
Turned westward, shaping in the steady clouds
Thy sands and high white cliffs!

My native Land!
Filled with the thought of thee this heart was proud,
Yea, mine eye swam with tears: that all the view
From sovran Brocken, woods and woody hills,
Floated away, like a departing dream,
Feeble and dim! Stranger, these impulses
Blame thou not lightly; nor will I profane,
With hasty judgement or injurious doubt,
That man's sublimer spirit, who can feel
That God is everywhere! the God who framed
Mankind to be one mighty family,
Himself our Father, and the World our Home.
1799

ODE TO TRANQUILLITY

Tranquillity! thou better name
Than all the family of Fame!
Thou ne'er wilt leave my riper age
To low intrigue, or factious rage;
For oh! dear child of thoughtful Truth,
To thee I gave my early youth,
And left the bark, and blest the steadfast shore,
Ere yet the tempest rose and scared me with its roar.

Who late and lingering seeks thy shrine,
On him but seldom, Power divine,
Thy spirit rests! Satiety
And Sloth, poor counterfeits of thee,
Mock the tired worldling. Idle hope
And dire remembrance interlope,
To vex the feverish slumbers of the mind:
The bubble floats before, the spectre stalks behind.

But me thy gentle hand will lead
At morning through the accustomed mead;
And in the sultry summer's heat
Will build me up a mossy seat;
And when the gust of Autumn crowds,
And breaks the busy moon-light clouds,
Thou best the thought canst raise, the heart attune,
Light as the busy clouds, calm as the gliding moon.

The feeling heart, the searching soul,
To thee I dedicate the whole!
And while within myself I trace
The greatness of some future race,
Aloof with hermit-eye I scan
The present works of present man –
A wild and dream-like trade of blood and guile,
Too foolish for a tear, too wicked for a smile!
1801

INSCRIPTION

For a fountain on a heath

This Sycamore, oft musical with bees –
Such tents the Patriarchs loved! O long unharmed
May all its aged boughs o'er-canopy
The small round basin, which this jutting stone
Keeps pure from falling leaves! Long may the Spring,
Quietly as a sleeping infant's breath,
Send up cold waters to the traveller
With soft and even pulse! Nor ever cease
Yon tiny cone of sand its soundless dance,
Which at the bottom, like a Fairy's page,
As merry and no taller, dances still,
Nor wrinkles the smooth surface of the Fount.
Here twilight is and coolness: here is moss,
A soft seat, and a deep and ample shade.
Thou may'st toil far and find no second tree.
Drink, Pilgrim, here; here rest! and if thy heart
Be innocent, here too shalt thou refresh
Thy Spirit, listening to some gentle sound,
Or passing gale or hum of murmuring bees!
1802

HYMN

Before sun-rise, in the Vale of Chamonix

Beside the Rivers, Arve and Arveiron, which have their sources in the foot of Mont Blanc, five conspicuous torrents rush down its sides; and within a few paces of the glaciers, the Gentiana Major grows in immense numbers, with its 'flowers of loveliest blue'.

Hast thou a charm to stay the morning star
In his steep course? So long he seems to pause
On thy bald awful head, O sovran Blanc,
The Arve and Arveiron at thy base
Rave ceaselessly; but thou, most awful Form!
Risest from forth thy silent sea of pines,
How silently! Around thee and above
Deep is the air and dark, substantial, black,
An ebon mass: methinks thou piercest it,
As with a wedge! But when I look again,
It is thine own calm home, thy crystal shrine,
Thy habitation from eternity!
O dread and silent Mount! I gazed upon thee,
Till thou, still present to the bodily sense,
Didst vanish from my thought: entranced in prayer
I worshipped the Invisible alone.

Yet, like some sweet beguiling melody,
So sweet, we know not we are listening to it,
Thou, the meanwhile, wast blending with my thought,
Yea, with my life and life's own secret joy;
Till the dilating Soul, enrapt, transfused,
Into the mighty vision passing – there
As in her natural form, swelled vast to Heaven!
Awake, my soul! not only passive praise
Thou owest! not alone these swelling tears,

Mute thanks and secret ecstasy! Awake,
Voice of sweet song! Awake, my heart, awake!
Green vales and icy cliffs, all join my Hymn.

Thou first and chief, sole sovereign of the Vale!
O struggling with the darkness all the night,
And visited all night by troops of stars,
Or when they climb the sky or when they sink:
Companion of the morning star at dawn,
Thyself Earth's rosy star, and of the dawn
Co-herald: wake, O wake, and utter praise!
Who sank thy sunless pillars deep in Earth?
Who filled thy countenance with rosy light?
Who made thee parent of perpetual streams?

And you, ye five wild torrents fiercely glad!
Who called you forth from night and utter death,
From dark and icy caverns called you forth,
Down those precipitous, black, jagged rocks,
For ever shattered and the same for ever?
Who gave you your invulnerable life,
Your strength, your speed, your fury, and your joy,
Unceasing thunder and eternal foam?
And who commanded (and the silence came),
Here let the billows stiffen, and have rest?

Ye ice-falls! ye that from the mountain's brow
Adown enormous ravines slope amain –
Torrents, methinks, that heard a mighty voice,
And stopped at once amid their maddest plunge!
Motionless torrents! silent cataracts!
Who made you glorious as the gates of Heaven
Beneath the keen full moon? Who bade the sun
Clothe you with rainbows? Who, with living flowers
Of loveliest blue, spread garlands at your feet? –

God! let the torrents, like a shout of nations,
Answer! and let the ice-plains echo, God!
God! sing ye meadow streams with gladsome voice!
Ye pine groves, with your soft and soul-like sounds!
And they too have a voice, yon piles of snow,
And in their perilous fall shall thunder, God!

Ye living flowers that skirt the eternal frost!
Ye wild goats sporting round the eagle's nest!
Ye eagles, play-mates of the mountain storm!
Ye lightnings, the dread arrows of the clouds!
Ye signs and wonders of the element!
Utter forth God, and fill the hills with praise!

Thou too, hoar Mount! with thy sky-pointing peaks,
Oft from whose feet the avalanche, unheard,
Shoots downward, glittering through the pure serene
Into the depth of clouds, that veil thy breast –
Thou too again, stupendous Mountain! thou
That as I raise my head, awhile bowed low
In adoration, upward from thy base
Slow travelling with dim eyes suffused with tears,
Solemnly seemest, like a vapoury cloud,
To rise before me – Rise, O ever rise,
Rise like a cloud of incense, from the Earth!
Thou kingly Spirit throned among the hills,
Thou dread ambassador from Earth to Heaven,
Great hierarch! tell thou the silent sky,
And tell the stars, and tell yon rising sun
Earth, with her thousand voices, praises God.
1802

ANSWER TO A CHILD'S QUESTION

Do you ask what the birds say? The sparrow, the dove,
The linnet and thrush say, 'I love and I love!'
In the winter they're silent – the wind is so strong;
What it says, I don't know, but it sings a loud song.
But green leaves, and blossoms, and sunny warm weather,
And singing, and loving – all come back together.
But the lark is so brimful of gladness and love,
The green fields below him, and the blue sky above,
That he sings, and he sings; and for ever sings he –
'I love my Love, and my Love loves me!'
1802

THE PAINS OF SLEEP

Ere on my bed my limbs I lay,
It hath not been my use to pray
With moving lips or bended knees;
But silently, by slow degrees,
My spirit I to Love compose,
In humble trust mine eye-lids close,
With reverential resignation,
No wish conceived, no thought exprest,
Only a sense of supplication;
A sense o'er all my soul imprest
That I am weak, yet not unblest,
Since in me, round me, every-where
Eternal strength and wisdom are.

But yester-night I prayed aloud
In anguish and in agony,
Up-starting from the fiendish crowd
Of shapes and thoughts that tortured me:
A lurid light, a trampling throng,
Sense of intolerable wrong,
And whom I scorned, those only strong!
Thirst of revenge, the powerless will
Still baffled, and yet burning still!
Desire with loathing strangely mixed
On wild or hateful objects fixed.
Fantastic passions! maddening brawl!
And shame and terror over all!
Deeds to be hid which were not hid,
Which all confused I could not know
Whether I suffered, or I did:
For all seemed guilt, remorse or woe,
My own or others still the same
Life-stifling fear, soul-stifling shame.

So two nights passed: the night's dismay
Saddened and stunned the coming day.
Sleep, the wide blessing, seemed to me
Distemper's worst calamity.
The third night, when my own loud scream
Had waked me from the fiendish dream,
O'ercome with sufferings strange and wild,
I wept as I had been a child;
And having thus by tears subdued
My anguish to a milder mood,
Such punishments, I said, were due
To natures deepliest stained with sin –
For aye entempesting anew
The unfathomable hell within,
The horror of their deeds to view,
To know and loathe, yet wish and do!
Such griefs with such men well agree,
But wherefore, wherefore fall on me?
To be beloved is all I need,
And whom I love, I love indeed.

1803

WHAT IS LIFE?

Resembles life what once was deem'd of light,
　　Too ample in itself for human sight?
An absolute self – an element ungrounded –
All that we see, all colours of all shade
　　By encroach of darkness made? –
Is very life by consciousness unbounded?
And all the thoughts, pains, joys of mortal breath,
A war-embrace of wrestling life and death?
1804

MY BAPTISMAL BIRTHDAY

God's child in Christ adopted, – Christ my all, –
What that earth boasts were not lost cheaply, rather
Than forfeit that blest name, by which I call
The Holy One, the Almighty God, my Father? –
Father! in Christ we live, and Christ in Thee –
Eternal Thou, and everlasting we.
The heir of Heaven, henceforth I fear not death:
In Christ I live! in Christ I draw the breath
Of the true life! – Let, then, earth, sea, and sky
Make war against me! On my front I show
Their mighty Master's seal. In vain they try
To end my life, that can but end its woe. –
Is that a deathbed where a Christian lies? –
Yes! but not his – 'tis Death itself that dies.

THE VISIONARY HOPE

Sad lot, to have no hope! Though lowly kneeling
He fain would frame a prayer within his breast,
Would fain entreat for some sweet breath of healing,
That his sick body might have ease and rest;
He strove in vain! the dull sighs from his chest
Against his will the stifling load revealing,
Though Nature forced; though like come captive guest,
Some royal prisoner at his conqueror's feast,
An alien's restless mood but half concealing,
The sternness on his gentle brow confessed,
Sickness within and miserable feeling:
Though obscure pangs made curses of his dreams,
And dreaded sleep, each night repelled in vain,
Each night was scattered by its own loud screams:
Yet never could his heart command, though fain,
One deep full wish to be no more in pain.

That Hope, which was his inward bliss and boast,
Which waned and died, yet ever near him stood,
Though changed in nature, wander where he would –
For Love's despair is but Hope's pining ghost!
For this one hope he makes his hourly moan,
He wishes and can wish for this alone!
Pierced, as with light from Heaven, before its gleams
(So the love-stricken visionary deems)
Disease would vanish, like a summer shower,
Whose dews fling sunshine from the noon-tide bower!
Or let it stay! yet this one Hope should give
Such strength that he would bless his pains and live.
1810

EPITAPH

Stop, Christian Passer-by! – Stop, child of God,
And read with gentle breast. Beneath this sod
A poet lies, or that which once seem'd he.
O, lift one thought in prayer for S. T. C.;
That he who many a year with toil of breath
Found death in life, may here find life in death!
Mercy for praise – to be forgiven for fame
He ask'd, and hoped, through Christ. Do thou the same!

1833

Prose

From
Essays in his own Times
1796 – 1800

DIGNITY AND SLAVERY

Wherein am I made worse by my ennobled neighbour? Do the childish titles of aristocracy detract from my domestic comforts, or prevent my intellectual acquisitions? But those institutions of society which should condemn me to the necessity of twelve hours' daily toil, would make my *soul* a slave, and sink the *rational* being in the mere animal. It is a mockery of our fellow creatures' wrongs to call them equal in rights, when by the bitter compulsion of their wants we make them inferior to us in all that can soften the heart, or dignify the understanding. Let us not say that this is the work of time – that it is impracticable at present, unless we each in our individual capacities do strenuously and perseveringly endeavour to diffuse among our domestics those comforts and that illumination which far beyond all political ordinances are the true equalizers of men.

We turn with pleasure to the contemplation of that small but glorious band, whom we may truly distinguish by the name of thinking and disinterested patriots. These are the men who have encouraged the sympathetic passions till they have become irresistible habits, and made their duty a necessary part of their self-interest, by the long-continued cultivation of that moral taste which derives our most exquisite pleasures from the contemplation of possible perfection, and proportionate pain from the perception of existing *depravation*. Accustomed to regard all the affairs of man as a process, they never hurry and they never pause. Theirs is not that

twilight of political knowledge which gives us just light enough to
place one foot before the other; as they advance the scene still opens
upon them, and they press right onward with a vast and various
landscape of existence around them. Calmness and energy mark all
their actions. Convinced that vice originates not in the man, but in
the surrounding circumstances; not in the heart, but in the under-
standing; he is hopeless concerning no one – to correct a vice or
generate a virtuous conduct he pollutes not his hands with the
scourge of coercion; but by endeavouring to alter the circumstances
would remove, or by strengthening the intellect, disarms, the
temptation.

WAR – 1

In former wars the victims of ambition had crowded to the standard
from the influence of national antipathies; but this powerful stimu-
lant has been so unceasingly applied, as to have well nigh produced
an exhaustion. What remains? Hunger. Over a recruiting place in
this city I have seen pieces of beef hung up to attract the half-
famished mechanic. It has been said that government, though not
the best preceptor of virtue, procures us security from the attack of
the lower orders. – Alas! why should the lower orders attack us, but
because they are brutalized by ignorance and rendered desperate by
want? And does government remove this ignorance by education?
And does not government increase their want by taxes? – Taxes
rendered necessary by those national assassinations called wars, and
by that worst corruption and perjury, which a reverend moralist has
justified under the soft title of 'secret influence'! The poor infant
born in an English or Irish hovel breathes indeed the air and partakes
of the light of Heaven; but of its other bounties he is disinherited.
The powers of intellect are given him in vain: to make him work like
a brute beast he is kept as ignorant as a brute beast. It is not possible
that this despised and oppressed man should behold the rich and

idle, without malignant envy. And if in the bitter cravings of hunger the dark tide of passions should swell, and the poor wretch rush from despair into guilt, then the government indeed assumes the right of punishment though it had neglected the duty of instruction, and hangs the victim for crimes to which its own wide-wasting follies and its own most sinful omissions had supplied the cause and the temptation. And yet how often have the fierce bigots of despotism told me that the poor are not to be pitied, however great their necessities: for if they be out of employ, the king wants men! They may be shipped off to the slaughter-house abroad, if they wish to escape a prison at home!

Fools! to commit robberies and get hanged, when they might fight for their king and country – yea, and have sixpence a day into the bargain!

THE DIFFUSION OF KNOWLEDGE

Such are the impediments to the diffusion of knowledge. The means by which Providence seems to be counteracting these impediments are:

First and principally, the progress of the Methodists, and other disciples of Calvinism. It has been a common remark, that implicit faith in mysteries prepares the mind for implicit obedience to tyranny. But this is plausible rather than just. Facts are against it. The most thorough-paced Republicans in the days of Charles the First were religious enthusiasts: and in the present day, a large majority among our sectaries are fervent in their zeal against political abuses. The truth seems to be, that superstition is unfavourable to civil freedom then only, when it teaches sensuality, as among atheists and pagans, and Mussulmen; or when it is in alliance with power and avarice, as in the religious establishments of Europe. In all other cases, to forego, even in solitude, the high pleasures which the human mind receives from the free exertion of its faculties, through the dread of an invisible spectator or the hope of a future reward, implies so great a conquest over the tyranny of the present impulse, and so large a power of self-government, that whoever is conscious of it, will be grateful for the existence of an external government no further than as it protects him from the attacks of others; which when that government omits to do, or when by promoting ignorance and depravity it produces the contrary effects, he is prepared to declare hostilities against it, and by the warmth of his feelings and the gregariousness of his nature is enabled to prosecute them more effectually, than a myriad of detached metaphysical systematizers. Besides, the very act of dissenting from established opinions must generate habits precursive to the love of freedom. Man begins to be free when he begins to examine. To this we may add, that men can hardly apply themselves with such perseverant zeal to the instruction and comforting of the poor, without feeling affection for them; and these feelings of love must necessarily lead to a blameless indignation against the authors of their complicated miseries. Nor should we forget, that however absurd their enthusiasm may be, yet if Methodism produce sobriety and domestic habits among the lower classes, it makes them susceptible of liberty; and this very enthusiasm does perhaps supersede the use of spirituous liquors, and bring on the same pleasing tumult of the brain without injuring the health or exhausting the wages. And although by the power of prejudice these sectaries may deduce from the Gospel doctrines which it does not contain, yet it is impossible that they should peruse the New Testament so frequently and with such attention, without perceiving and remembering the precepts which it does contain. Yes! they shudder with pious horror at the idea of defending by famine, and fire, and blood, that religion which teaches its followers – 'If thine enemy hunger, feed him; if he thirst, give him drink: *for by so doing thou shalt melt him into repentance.*'

Secondly, the institution of large manufactories; in many of which it is the custom for a newspaper to be regularly read, and sometimes larger publications. Which party they adopt is of little comparative consequence! Men always serve the cause of freedom by *thinking*, even though their first reflections may lead them to oppose it. And on account of these men, whose passions are frequently inflamed by drunkenness, the friends of rational and progressive liberty may review with diminished indignation two recent acts of parliament, which, though breaches of the constitution, and under pretence of protecting the *head* of the state, evidently passed to prevent our cutting off an enormous *wen* that grows upon it (I mean the system of secret influence), yet will not have been useless if they should render the language of political publications more cool and guarded, or even confine us for a while to the teaching of first principles, or the diffusion of that general knowledge which should be the basis or substratum of politics.

Thirdly, the number of book societies established in almost every town and city of the kingdom; and,

Fourthly, the increasing experience of the dreadful effects of war and corruption.

MORAL INDIGNATION AND SELF-INTEREST

There is observable among the many a false and bastard sensibility that prompts them to remove those evils, and those evils alone, which by hideous spectacle or clamorous outcry are present to their senses, and disturb their selfish enjoyments. Other miseries, though equally certain and far more horrible, they not only do not endeavour to remedy – they support, they fatten on them. Provided the dunghill be not before their parlour window, they are well content to know that it exists, and that it is the hot-bed of their pestilent luxuries. – To this grievous failing we must attribute the frequency of wars, and the continuance of the slave trade. The merchant finds no argument against it in his ledger: the citizen at the crowded feast is not nauseated by the stench and filth of the slave-vessel – the fine lady's nerves are not shattered by the shrieks! She sips a beverage sweetened with human blood, even while she is weeping over the refined sorrows of Werther or of Clementina. Sensibility is not benevolence. Nay, by making us tremblingly alive to trifling misfortunes, it frequently prevents it, and induces effeminate and cowardly selfishness. Our own sorrows, like the Princes of Hell in Milton's Pandemonium, sit enthroned 'bulky and vast': while the miseries of our fellow creatures dwindle into pigmy forms, and are crowded, an innumerable multitude, into some dark corner of the heart. There is one criterion by which we may always distinguish benevolence from mere sensibility – benevolence impels to action, and is accompanied by self-denial.

COMMERCE AND THE HUMAN SPIRIT

But on the supposition that by a perpetual continuance of the war, or by a restoration of despotism, or by any other means, we could be and remain the monopolists of the commerce of Europe, is it quite ascertained that it would be a real *national* advantage? Is it quite certain that the condition and morals of the lower and more numerous classes would not be progressively deteriorated? Is it quite certain that it would not give such a superiority to the moneyed interest of the country over the landed, as might be fatal to our constitution? Has not the hereditary possession of landed estate been proved, by experience, to generate dispositions equally favourable to loyalty and established freedom? Has not the same experience proved that the moneyed men are far more malleable materials? that ministers find more and more easy ways of obliging them, and that they are more willing to go with a minister through evil and good? Our commerce has been, it is said, nearly trebled since the war; is the nation at large the happier? Have the schemes of internal navigation, and of rendering waste lands useful, proceeded with their former energy? Or have not loans and other ministerial job-work created injurious and perhaps vicious objects for moneyed speculations? – And what mean these committees for the labouring poor? These numerous soup establishments? These charities so kindly and industriously set on foot through the whole kingdom? All these are highly honourable to the rich of this country! But are they equally honourable to the nation at large? – Is that a genuine prosperity, in which healthy labourers are commonly styled 'the labouring *poor*', and industrious manufacturers obliged to be fed, like Roman clients, or Neapolitan Lazzaroni?

Finally, commerce is the blessing and pride of this country. It is necessary, as a stimulus to the agriculture which sustains, and as the support of the navy which defends, us; but let us not forget that commerce is still no otherwise valuable than as the means to an end, and ought not itself to become the end, to which nobler and more inherent blessings are to be forced into subserviency.

INTERNATIONAL RELATIONS

The French have broken treaties; we, therefore, can make no treaties with the French. But did not all our allies, at the commencement of the war, enter into solemn treaties not to lay down arms but by mutual consent? And did they not all break this treaty? What is the whole history of modern Europe, but a succession of wars, originating in broken treaties? It is absurd to apply that against a treaty of peace with one country, which does not apply against even a treaty of alliance with all other countries; and yet, as Mr Fox well observed, the moral character of our friends and fellow labourers is assuredly of more importance to us than that of those whom we wish only not to be our enemies. Let any man mention any act of folly, treachery, or oppression in the French Republic, and we pledge ourselves to find a *fellow* to it in our own allies, or in the history of the line of princes, upon the restoration of whom an honourable peace is now made to depend. To us the turn of the debate on Monday is a matter of hope and exultation. The harangues of the ministers were absolute confessions of weakness. Long and tedious details of French aggressions, which, if they had been as fair and accurate as they were false and partial, would still prove nothing; violent personalities on Bonaparte, and as violent panegyrics on the superior science, talents, and humanity of the conqueror of Warsaw and Ismail; and the old delusive calculations about French resources, calculations always accompanied by prophecies, which prophecies have been always, even to a laughable degree, falsified: these formed the substance and contents of the ministerial orations. More than one half of Mr Pitt's speech was consumed in the old re-repeated tale of the origin of the war. This can be nothing more than an appeal to passion. For let us suppose for a moment that we, and not the French, were the aggressors, the unprovoked aggressors; that they were innocent, and we guilty – yet how would this affect the subject of peace? Is any man so contemptibly ignorant of the rules and first foundations of State morality, as to affirm that because our Ministers had entered into a war knavishly, therefore the people were bound in honour or honesty to conclude a peace ruinously? The interest of nations, the true interest, is and ought to be the sole guide in national concerns; and all besides is puerile declamation, only serviceable as covering a defeat, and preventing the appearance of an absolute rout, such as would have been implied in silence. What two nations were ever at war, and did not obstinately charge the aggression, each on the other? Has not this been matter of course since the time that the introduction of the Christian religion has made the governors of mankind afraid to state conquest or glory as their motives? And to adduce this as a political reason against the propriety of concluding a peace, or even of entering on a negotiation!

WAR – 2

The Crusades were as favourable in their effects as they were honourable in their causes. Then first did Europe feel, and become conscious of the blessing of a common religion, and of civil institutions, differing only as the branches of one family, '*qualis decet esse sororum*'. The warriors brought back from the holy land imaginations highly excited, minds enlarged by the contemplation of a scenery and of customs so new to them, and manners polished beyond the experience of former ages. A new era commenced in the world; a new sun rose on our social habits, on the tone of governments, and on the nature of our literature. The monkish legend and obsolete miracle gave way to Knights, the Giants, and Genii; and enthusiasm and imagination, mutually feeding each other, were brought to act on the side of gentleness and public justice. Unless therefore it shall be admitted that Suwarrow and his Russians have returned home poets and gentlemen; or that our Bond Street officers have been transmuted, by the alchemy of our expeditions, into the chaste, gentle and sober knights of ancient chivalry; let us call the present war anything: ONLY NOT A CRUSADE.

These Crusades were likewise the parents of all the freedom which now exists in Europe. The pecuniary distresses of the monarchs and nobles compelled them to part with many and various privileges, the anarchy which prevailed during their absence procured to the lower classes many others. Commerce was diverted from the Venetian and Genoese monopolizers; and there began to arise in all countries, but more especially in England, that greatest blessing and ornament of human nature: an important and respectable middle class. The monarch became more an officer, and less a person; the nobility were seen gradually to draw nearer to the class of the people; and long before the first dawn of religious reformation, the poetic genius imported from the last had prepared the way for it, by continued and successful satires on the absurdities and crimes of the priesthood. Unless therefore it be admitted that the *direct* object of the present war is to lay the foundations of a greater freedom than we before enjoyed; unless it be admitted that it has tended to prevent commerce from being a monopoly of one nation; unless it be granted, that it, namely this present war, spite of the assessed and income taxes, is peculiarly favourable to the increase and permanence of a middle class; that it militates against all attachment to kings as persons, and nobles as *privileged* classes; and to the Roman Catholic superstitions, as absurdities; unless all this be conceded by the friends of Freedom, let them call the present war anything: ONLY NOT A CRUSADE.

KNOWLEDGE AND EDUCATION

… Whatever inconvenience may have arisen from the commonness of education, can only be removed by rendering it universal. But that alone is worthy the name, which does indeed educe the faculties and form the habits; and reading and writing we should place among the *means* of education, instead of regarding it as the *end*. At no time and in no rank of life can knowledge be made our prime object without injury to the understanding, and certain perversion of those moral institutions, to the cultivation of which it must be instrumental and subservient, or, vapour and nothingness as the human intellect is, separated from that better light which lifts and transpierces it, even that which it has will be taken away. The neglect of this truth is the worm at the root of certain modern improvements in the modes of teaching, in comparison with which we have been called on to despise our great public schools

> 'In whose halls are hung
> Armoury of the invincible knights of old'

and have been instructed how to metamorphose children into prodigies; and prodigies with a vengeance have I known thus produced, prodigies of self-conceit, shallowness, arrogance, and infidelity. Instead of storing the memory, during the period when the memory is the predominant faculty, with facts for the after-exercise of the judgement, and instead of awakening by the noblest models the fond and unmixed *love* and *admiration*, which is the natural and graceful temper of early youth, these nurslings of improved pedagogy are taught to dispute and deride, to suspect all but their own and their lecturer's wisdom, and to hold nothing sacred from their contempt but their own contemptible arrogance; boy graduates in all the technical and all the dirty passions and impudence of anonymous criticism.

PHILOSOPHY AND SOCIETY

In every state not wholly barbarous, a philosophy, good or bad, there must be. However slightingly it may be the fashion to talk of speculation and theory, as opposed (sillily and nonsensically opposed) to practice, it would not be difficult to prove, that such as is the existing spirit of speculation, during any given period, such will be the spirit and tone of the religion, legislation, and morals, nay, even of the fine arts, the manners, and the fashions. Nor is this the less true, because the great majority of men live like bats, but in twilight, and know and feel the philosophy of their age only by its reflections and refractions.

CRIME AND PUNISHMENT

We have just read in a provincial paper a list of the petty culprits who had received sentence at a County Sessions. – We do not mention names: for our remarks apply to the laws, and not to the individuals who exercised their discretion within the bounds permitted by them. In this list we see one man imprisoned twelve months for stealing a sack of coals; a young woman, for stealing six loaves, sentenced to six months' imprisonment, *and to be whipped*; and three other females for petty thefts, one to six, and the others to three months' imprisonment, *and to be whipped*; while a man and a woman, convicted of having long kept an *infamous brothel* in a *country town*, were sentenced to two months' imprisonment, and to be fined ONE SHILLING.

Now let any thinking head and feeling heart consider the nature and consequences of the offence last mentioned. Think of such a house in such a place, as a small swamp, whose pestilential vapours extend as far as the remotest habitation of those who attend its weekly markets. Think of the early corruption and *heart-hardening* of the apprentices and other youths of the town and vicinity; of the recruits for prostitution raised from the servant maids, and other still more unprotected females; of the diseases, sapping manhood, and alas! so often carried into families, and re-appearing in the second and third generation in the form of scrofula, consumption, and mania! – and then weigh in the balance of reason a hundred petty thefts with the guilt of this one crime! We well know that laws cannot be proportioned to the moral guilt of actions, but must take in, as a most important guide, the difficulty and necessity of prevention: but we likewise know that laws can never *outrage* the proportions established by the conscience without either baffling themselves or degrading the public morals.

This, however, is not all that pained us. We were in hopes that with the progressive refinement and increased tenderness of private and domestic feelings (in which we are doubtless superior to our ancestors, whatever the average of virtue may be), this unmanly practice of scourging females had gradually become obsolete, and placed among the *Inusitata* of the law dictionary. It is not only the female herself who yet, if not already a miscreant, must needs (to use a far softer phrase than our feelings would prompt) be grievously injured in the first sources and primary impulses of female worth – for who will deny that the infamy which would attend a young woman from having being stripped naked under the lash of a townsman, would be incomparably greater, and have burnt deeper in, than what would accrue from her having been detected in stealing half a dozen loaves? We are not shocked for the female only, but for the inflictor, and at the unmanliness of the punishment itself. Good God! how is it possible, that man, *born of woman*, could go through the office? O never let it be forgotten, either by the framers or dispensers of criminal law, that the stimulus of shame, like some powerful medicines, if administered in too large a dose, becomes a deadly narcotic poison to the moral patient! Never let it be forgotten that every human being bears in himself that indelible something which belongs equally to the whole species, as well as that particular modification of it which individualizes him: that *the* woman is still *woman*, and however she may have debased herself, yet that we should still show some respect, still feel some reverence, if not for her sake, yet in awe of that Being, who saw good to stamp in her his own image, and forbade it ever, in this life at least, to be utterly erased.

From
The Friend
1809 – 1810

TOLERATION

From this hint concerning Toleration, we may pass by an easy transition to the perhaps still more interesting subject of Tolerance. And here I fully coincide with Frederic H. Jacobi, that the only true spirit of Tolerance consists in our conscientious toleration of each other's intolerance. Whatever pretends to be more than this, is either the unthinking cant of fashion, or the soul-palsying narcotic of moral and religious indifference. All of us without exception, in the same mode though not in the same degree, are necessarily subjected to the risk of mistaking positive opinions for certainty and clear insight. From this yoke we cannot free ourselves, but by ceasing to be men; and this too not in order to transcend, but to sink below, our human nature. For if in one point of view it be the mulct of our fall, and of the corruption of our will; it is equally true that, contemplated from another point, it is the price and consequence of our progressiveness. To him who is compelled to pace to and fro within the high walls and in the narrow courtyard of a prison, all objects may appear clear and distinct. It is the traveller journeying onward, full of heart and hope, with an ever-varying horizon, on the boundless plain, that is liable to mistake clouds for mountains, and the mirage of drought for an expanse of refreshing waters.

But notwithstanding this deep conviction of our general fallibility, and the most vivid recollection of my own, I dare avow with the German philosopher, that as far as opinions, and not motives, principles, and not men, are concerned; I neither am *tolerant*, nor wish to be regarded as such. According to my judgement, it is mere ostentation, or a poor trick that hypocrisy plays with the cards of nonsense, when a man makes protestation of being perfectly tolerant in respect of all principles, opinions, and persuasions, those alone excepted which render the holders intolerant. For he either means to say by this, that he is utterly indifferent towards all truth, and finds nothing so insufferable as the persuasion of there being any such mighty value or importance attached to the possession of the truth as should give a marked preference to any one conviction above any other; or else he means nothing, and amuses himself with articulating the pulses of the air instead of inhaling it in the more healthful and profitable exercise of yawning. That which doth not *withstand*, hath *itself* no standing place. To *fill* a station is to exclude or repel others – and this is not less the definition of moral, than of material, *solidity*. We *live* by continued acts of defence, that involve a sort of offensive warfare. But a man's principles, on which he grounds his Hope and his Faith, are the life of his life. We live by Faith, says the philosophic Apostle; and Faith without principles is but a flattering phrase for wilful positiveness, or fanatical bodily sensation. Well, and of good right therefore, do we maintain with more zeal than we should defend body or estate, a deep and inward conviction, which is as the moon to us; and like the moon with all its massy shadows and deceptive gleams, it yet lights us on our way, poor travellers as we are, and benighted pilgrims. With all its spots and changes and temporary eclipses, with all its vain haloes and bedimming vapours, it yet reflects the light that is to rise on us, which even now is *rising*, though intercepted from our immediate view by the mountains that enclose and frown over the vale of our mortal life.

This again is the mystery and the dignity of our human nature, that we cannot give up our reason without giving up at the same time our individual personality. For that must appear to each man to be *his* reason which produces in him the highest sense of certainty; and yet it is *not* reason, except so far as it is of universal validity and obligatory on all mankind. There is one heart for the whole mighty mass of humanity, and every pulse in each particular vessel strives to beat in concert with it. He who asserts that truth is of no importance except in the signification of sincerity, confounds sense with madness, and the word of God with a dream. If the power of reasoning be the gift of the supreme Reason, that we be sedulous, yea, and *militant* in the endeavour to reason aright, is his implied command. But what is of permanent and essential interest to one man must needs be so to all, in proportion to the means and opportunities of each. Woe to him by whom these are neglected, and double woe to him by whom they are withholden; for he robs at once himself and his neighbour. That man's soul is not dear to himself, to whom the souls of his brethren are not dear. As far as they can be influenced by him, they are parts and properties of his own soul, their faith his faith, their errors his burthen, their righteousness and bliss his righteousness and his reward – and of their guilt and misery his own will be the echo. As much as I love my fellow men, so much and no more will I be *intolerant* of their heresies and unbelief – and I will honour and hold forth the right hand of fellowship to every individual who is equally intolerant of that which he conceives such in me. – We will both exclaim: 'I know not what antidotes among the complex views, impulses and circumstances, that form your moral being, God's gracious providence may have vouchsafed to you against the serpent fang of this error – but it is a viper, and its poison deadly, although through higher influences some men may take the reptile to their bosom, and remain unstung.'

SELF-KNOWLEDGE

How can a truth, new to us, be made our own without examination and self-questioning – any new truth, I mean, that relates to the properties of the mind, and its various faculties and affections? But whatever demands effort, requires time. Ignorance seldom *vaults* into knowledge, but passes into it through an intermediate state of obscurity, even as night into day through twilight. All speculative truths begin with a postulate, even the truths of geometry. They all suppose an act of the will; for in the moral being lies the source of the intellectual. The first step to knowledge, or rather the previous condition of all insight into truth, is to dare commune with our very and permanent self.

DREAMS, VISIONS, GHOSTS AND WITCHCRAFT

I have long wished to devote an entire work to the subject of dreams, visions, ghosts and witchcraft, in which I might first give, and then endeavour to explain, the most interesting and best attested fact of each which has come within my knowledge, either from books or from personal testimony. I might then explain in a more satisfactory way the mode in which our thoughts, in states of morbid slumber, become at times perfectly *dramatic* (for in certain sorts of dreams the dullest wight becomes a Shakespeare), and by what law the *form* of the vision appears to talk to us its own thoughts in a voice as audible as the shape is visible; and this too often-times in connected trains, and not seldom even with a concentration of power which may easily impose on the soundest judgements, uninstructed in the *optics* and *acoustics* of the inner sense, for revelations and gifts of prescience. In aid of the present case, I will only remark that it would appear incredible to persons not accustomed to these subtle notices of self-observation, what small and remote resemblances, what mere hints of likeness from some real external object, especially if the shape be aided by colour, will suffice to make a vivid thought consubstantiate with the real object, and derive from it an outward perceptibility. Even when we are broad awake, it we are in anxious expectation, how often will not the most confused sounds of nature be heard by us as articulate sounds? For instance, the babbling of a brook will appear for a moment the voice of a friend, for whom we are waiting, calling out our own names et cetera. A short meditation, therefore, on the great law of the imagination, that a likeness in part tends to become a likeness of the whole, will make it not only conceivable but probable, that the inkstand itself, and the dark-coloured stone on the wall, which Luther perhaps had never till then noticed, might have a considerable influence in the production of the fiend, and of the hostile act by which his obtrusive visit was repelled.

A lady once asked me if I believed in ghosts and apparitions. I answered with truth and simplicity: *No, madam! I have seen far too many myself.* I have indeed a whole memorandum book filled with records of these phenomena, many of them interesting as facts and data for psychology, and affording some valuable materials for a theory of perception and its dependence on the memory and imagination.

THE LAW AND THE MIND

Strength may be met with strength; the power of inflicting pain may be baffled by the pride of endurance; the eye of rage may be answered by the stare of defiance, or the downcast look of dark and revengeful resolve; and with all this there is an outward and deter-mined object to which the mind can attach its passions and purposes, and bury its own disquietudes in the full occupation of the senses. But who dares struggle with an *invisible* combatant? with an enemy which exists and makes us know its existence – but *where* it is, we ask in vain. No space contains it – time promises no control over it – it has no ear for my threats – it has no subtance that my hands can grasp, or my weapons find vulnerable – it commands and cannot be commanded – it acts and is insusceptible of my reaction – the more I strive to subdue it, the more am I compelled to think of it – and the more I think of it, the more do I find it to possess a reality out of myself, and not to be a phantom of my own imagination; that all but the most abandoned men acknowledge its authority, and that the whole strength and majesty of my country are pledged to support it; and yet that for *me* its power is the same with that of my own permanent self, and that all the choice which is permitted to me consists in having it for my guardian angel or my avenging fiend! This is the spirit of law! the lute of Amphion, the harp of Orpheus! This is the true necessity, which compels man into the social state, now and always, by a still-beginning, never-ceasing force of moral cohesion.

Thus is man to be governed, and thus only can he be governed.

FREEDOM

Who then shall dare prescribe a law of moral action for any rational being, which does not flow immediately from that Reason, which is the fountain of all morality? Or how without breach of conscience can we limit or coerce the powers of a free agent, except by coincidence with that law in his own mind, which is at once the cause, the condition, and the measure of his free agency? Man must be *free*; or to what purpose was he made a spirit of reason, and not a machine of instinct? Man must *obey*; or wherefore has he a conscience? The powers, which create this difficulty, contain its solution likewise: for *their* service is perfect freedom. And whatever law or system of law compels any other service, disennobles our nature, leagues itself with the animal against the godlike, kills in us the very principle of joyous well-doing, and fights against humanity.

CONTROVERSY

And finally, and above all, let it be remembered by both parties, and indeed by controversialists on all subjects, that every speculative error which boasts a multitude of advocates, has its *golden* as well as its dark side; that there is always some truth connected with it, the exclusive attention to which has misled the understanding, some moral beauty which has given it charms for the heart. Let it be remembered that no assailant of an error can reasonably hope to be listened to by its advocates, who has not proved to them that he has seen the disputed subject in the same point of view, and is capable of contemplating it with the same feelings as themselves (for why should we abandon a cause at the persuasions of one who is ignorant of the reasons which have attached us to it?). Let it be remembered that to write, however ably, merely to convince those who are already convinced, displays but the courage of a boaster; and in any subject to rail against the evil before we have enquired for the good, and to exasperate the passions of those who think with us, by caricaturing the opinions and blackening the motives of our antagonists, is to make the understanding the pander of the passions; and even though we should have defended the right cause, to gain for ourselves ultimately from the good and the wise no other praise than the supreme Judge awarded to the friends of Job for their partial and uncharitable defence of his justice: 'My wrath is kindled against you, for ye have not spoken of me *rightfully*.'

TRUE FAITH

Just and generous actions may proceed from bad motives, and both may, and often do, originate *in parts*, and, as it were, *fragments* of our nature. A lascivious man may sacrifice half his estate to rescue his friend from prison, for he is constitutionally sympathetic, and the better part of his nature happened to be uppermost. The same man shall afterwards exert the same disregard of money in an attempt to seduce that friend's wife or daughter. But faith is a *total* act of the soul: it is the *whole* state of the mind, or it is not at all! and in this consists its power, as well as its exclusive worth.

MIRACLES

There are spiritual truths which must derive their evidence from within, which whoever rejects 'neither will he believe though a man were to rise from the dead' to confirm them. And under the Mosaic law a miracle in attestation of a false doctrine subjected the miracle worker to death: and whether the miracle was really or only seemingly supernatural, makes no difference in the present argument, its power of convincing, whatever that power may be, whether great or small, depending on the fulness of the belief in its miraculous nature. *Est quibus esse videtur.* Or rather, that I may express the same position in a form less likely to offend, is not a true *efficient* conviction of a moral truth, is not the creating of a new heart, which collects the energies of a man's whole being in the focus of the conscience, the one essential miracle, the same and of the same evidence to the ignorant and the learned, which no superior skill can counterfeit, human or demoniacal? Is it not emphatically that leading of the Father, without which no man can come to Christ? Is it not that implication of doctrine in the miracle and of miracle in the doctrine, which is the bridge of communication between the senses and the soul? – That predisposing warmth which renders the understanding susceptible of the specific impression from the historic, and from all other outward seals of testimony? Is not this the one infallible criterion of miracles, by which a man can know whether they be of God? The abhorrence in which the most savage or barbarous tribes hold witchcraft, in which however their belief is so intense as even to control the springs of life – is not this abhorrence of witchcraft under so full a conviction of its reality a proof, how little of divine, how little fitting to our nature, a miracle is, when insulated from spiritual truths, and disconnected from religion as its end? What then can we think of a theological theory, which adopting a scheme of prudential legality, common to it with 'the sty of Epicurus', as far at least as the *springs* of moral action are concerned, makes its whole *religion* consist in the belief of miracles! As well might the poor African prepare for himself a fetish by plucking out the eyes from the eagle or the lynx, and enshrining the same, worship in them the power of vision. As the tenet of professed Christians (I speak of the principle not of the men, whose hearts will always more or less correct the errors of their understandings) it is even more absurd, and the pretext for such a religion more inconsistent than the religion itself. For they profess to derive from it their whole faith in that futurity, which if they had not previously believed on the evidence of their own consciences, of Moses and the Prophets, they are assured by the great Founder and Object of Christianity, that neither will they believe it, in any spiritual and profitable sense, though a man should rise from the dead.

For myself, I cannot resist the conviction, built on particular and general history, that the extravagances of Antinomianism and Solifidianism are little more than the counteractions to this Christian paganism: the play, as it were, of antagonist muscles. The feelings will set up their standard against the understanding, whenever the understanding has renounced its allegiance to the reason: and what is faith but the personal realization of the reason by its union with the will? If we would drive out the demons of fanaticism from the people, we must begin by exercising the spirit of Epicureanism in the higher ranks, and restore to the teachers the true Christian *enthusiasm*, the vivifying influences of the altar, the censer, and the sacrifice. They must neither be ashamed of, nor disposed to explain away, the articles of prevenient and auxiliary grace, nor the necessity of being born again to the life from which our nature had become apostate. They must administer indeed the necessary medicines to the sick, the motives of fear as well as of hope; but they must not withhold from them the idea of health, or conceal from them that the medicines for the sick are not the diet of the healthy. Nay, they must make it a part of the curative process to induce the patient, on the first symptoms of recovery, to look forward with prayer and aspiration to that state, in which *perfect love shutteth out fear*. Above all, they must not seek to make the mysteries of faith what the world calls *rational* by theories of original sin and redemption borrowed analogically from the imperfection of human law courts and the coarse contrivances of state expedience.

MORALITY

As long as the spirit of philosophy reigns in the learned and highest class, and that of religion in all classes, a tendency to blend and unite will be found in all objects of pursuit, and the whole discipline of mind and manners will be calculated in relation to the worth of the agents. With the prevalence of sophistry, when the pure will (if indeed the existence of a will be admitted in any other sense than as the temporary main current in the wide gust-eddying stream of our desires and aversions) is ranked among the *means* to an alien end, instead of being itself the one absolute end, in the participation of which all other things are worthy to be called good, commences the epoch of division and separation. Things are rapidly improved, persons as rapidly deteriorated; and for an indefinite period the powers of the aggregate increase, as the strength of the individual declines. Still, however, sciences may be estranged from philosophy, the practical from the speculative, and *one* of the two at least may remain. Music may be divided from poetry, and *both* may continue to exist, though with diminished influence. But religion and morals cannot be disjoined without the destruction of both: and that this does not take place to the full extent, we owe to the frequency with which both take shelter in the heart, and that men are always better or worse than the maxims which they adopt or concede.

THE ART OF METHOD

From Shakespeare to Plato, from the philosophic poet to the poetic philosopher, the transition is easy, and the road is crowded with illustrations of our present subject. For of Plato's works, the larger and more valuable portion have all one common end, which comprehends and shines through the particular purpose of each several dialogue; and this is to establish the sources, to evolve the principles, and exemplify the art of METHOD. This is the clue, without which it would be difficult to exculpate the noblest productions of the divine philosopher from the charge of being tortuous and labyrinthine in their progress, and unsatisfactory in their ostensible results. The latter indeed appear not seldom to have been drawn for the purpose of starting a new problem, rather than that of solving the one proposed as the subject of the previous discussion. But with the clear insight that the purpose of the writer is not so much to establish any particular truth, as to remove the obstacles, the continuance of which is preclusive of all truth, the whole scheme assumes a different aspect, and justifies itself in all its dimensions. We see that to open anew a well of springing water, not to cleanse the stagnant tank, or fill, bucket by bucket, the leaden cistern; that the EDUCATION of the intellect, by awakening the principle and *method* of self-development, was his proposed object, not any specific information that can be *conveyed* into it from without: not to assist in storing the passive mind with the various sorts of knowledge most in request, as if the human soul were a mere repository or banqueting room, but to place it in such relations of circumstance as should gradually excite the germinal power that craves no knowledge but what it can take up into itself, what it can appropriate, and reproduce in fruits of its own. To shape, to dye, to paint over, and to mechanize the mind, he resigned, as their proper trade, to the sophists, against whom he waged open and unremitting war.

From
Aids to Reflection
1825

APHORISM I

In philosophy equally as in poetry, it is the highest and most useful prerogative of genius to produce the strongest impressions of novelty, while it rescues admitted truths from the neglect caused by the very circumstance of their universal admission. Extremes meet. Truths, of all others the most awful and interesting, are too often considered as *so* true, that they lose all the power of truth, and lie bed-ridden in the dormitory of the soul, side by side with the most despised and exploded errors.

APHORISM II

There is one sure way of giving freshness and importance to the most *commonplace* maxims – that of *reflecting* on them in direct reference to our own state and conduct, to our own past and future being.

APHORISM III

To restore a commonplace truth to its first *uncommon* lustre, you need only *translate* it into action. But to do this, you must have *reflected* on its truth.

APHORISM IX

Life is the one universal soul, which, by virtue of the enlivening Breath, and the informing Word, all organized bodies have in common, each *after its kind*. This, therefore, all animals possess, and man as an animal. But, in addition to this, God transfused into man a higher gift, and specially imbreathed – even a living (that is, self-subsisting) soul, a soul having its life in itself. 'And man became a living soul.' He did not merely *possess* it, he *became* it. It was his proper *being*, his truest *self*, *the* man *in* the man. None then, not one of human kind, so poor and destitute, but there is provided for him, even in his present state, *a house not built with hands*. Aye, and spite of the philosophy (falsely so called) which mistakes the causes, the conditions, and the occasions of our becoming *conscious* of certain truths and realities for the truths and realities themselves – a house gloriously furnished. Nothing is wanted but the eye, which is the light of this house, the light which is the eye of this soul. This *seeing* light, this *enlightening* eye, is Reflection. It is more, indeed, than is ordinarily meant by that word; but it is what a Christian ought to mean by it, and to know too, whence it first came, and still continues to come – of what light even this light is *but* a reflection. This, too, is Thought; and all thought is but unthinking that does not flow out of this, or tend towards it.

APHORISM XI

An hour of solitude passed in sincere and earnest prayer, or the conflict with, and conquest over, a single passion or 'subtle *bosom* sin', will teach us more of thought, will more effectually awaken the *faculty*, and form the *habit*, of reflection, than a year's study in the schools without them.

APHORISM XII

In a world, the opinions of which are drawn from outside shows, many things may be *paradoxical* (that is, contrary to the common notion) and nevertheless true: nay, *because* they are true. How should it be otherwise, as long as the imagination of the Worldling is wholly occupied by surfaces, while the Christian's thoughts are fixed on the substance, that which *is* and abides, and which, *because* it is the substance, the outward senses cannot recognize. Tertullian had good reason for his assertion, that the simplest Christian (if indeed a Christian) knows more than the most accomplished irreligious philosopher.

APHORISM XIII

Never yet did there exist a full faith in the Divine Word (by whom *light*, as well as immortality, was brought into the world), which did not expand the intellect, while it purified the heart; which did not multiply the aims and objects of the understanding, while it fixed and simplified those of the desires and passions.

Comment

If acquiescence without insight; if warmth without light; if an immunity from doubt, given and guaranteed by a resolute ignorance; if the habit of *taking for granted* the words of a catechism, remembered or forgotten; if a mere *sensation* of positiveness substituted — I will not say, for the *sense* of *certainty*; but — for that calm assurance, the very means and conditions of which it supersedes; if a belief that seeks the darkness, and yet strikes no root, immovable as the limpet from the rock, and, like the limpet, fixed there by mere force of adhesion; if these suffice to make men Christians, in what sense could the Apostle affirm that believers receive, not indeed worldly wisdom, that comes to nought, but the wisdom of God, that we might *know and comprehend* the things that are freely given to us of God? On what grounds could he denounce the sincerest *fervour* of spirit as *defective*, where it does not likewise bring forth fruits in the Understanding?

APHORISM XXV

Woe to the man who will believe neither power, freedom nor morality; because he nowhere finds either entire, or unmixed with sin, thraldom and infirmity. In the natural and intellectual realms, we distinguish what we cannot separate; and in the moral world, we must distinguish *in order to* separate. Yea, in the clear distinction of good from evil the process of separation commences.

Comment

It was customary with religious men in former times, to make a rule of taking every morning some text, or aphorism, for their occasional meditation during the day, and thus to fill up the intervals of their attention to business. I do not point it out for imitation, as knowing too well, how apt these self-imposed rules are to degenerate into superstition or hollowness; otherwise I would have recommended the following as the first exercise.

APHORISM XXVI

It is a dull and obtuse mind that must divide in order to distinguish; but it is a still worse that distinguishes in order to divide. In the former, we may contemplate the source of superstition and idolatry; in the latter, of schism, heresy, and a seditious and sectarian spirit.

From
Confessions of an Inquiring Spirit
1840

SCRIPTURES

'*Curse ye Meroz,*' said the angel of the Lord, '*curse ye bitterly the inhabitants thereof,*' sang Deborah. Was it that she called to mind any personal wrongs – rapine or insult – that she or the house of Lapidoth had received from Jabin or Sisera? No; she had dwelt under her palm tree in the depth of the mountain. But she was a *mother in Israel*; and with a mother's heart, and with the vehemency of a mother's and a patriot's love, she had shot the light of love from her eyes, and poured the blessings of love from her lips, on the people that had *jeoparded their lives unto the death* against the oppressors; and the bitterness, awakened and borne aloft by the same love, she precipitated in curses on the selfish and coward recreants who *came not to the help of the Lord, to the help of the Lord, against the mighty*.

As long as I have the image of Deborah before my eyes, and while I throw myself back into the age, country, circumstances, of this Hebrew Boudicca in the not-yet-tamed chaos of the spiritual creation; as long as I contemplate the impassioned, high-souled, heroic woman in all the prominence and individuality of will and character – I feel as if I were among the first ferments of the great affections, the pro-plastic waves of the microcosmic chaos, swelling up against – and yet towards – the outspread wings of the Dove that lies brooding on the troubled waters. So long all is well, all replete with instruction and example. In the fierce and inordinate I am made to know and be grateful for the clearer and purer radiance which

93

shines on a Christian's paths, neither blunted by the preparatory veil, nor crimsoned in its struggle through the all-enwrapping mist of the world's ignorance: whilst in the self-oblivion of these heroes of the Old Testament, their elevation above all low and individual interests, above all, in the entire and vehement devotion of their total being to the service of their divine Master, I find a lesson of humility, a ground of humiliation, and a shaming, yet rousing, example of faith and fealty.

But let me once be persuaded that all these heart-awakening utterances of human hearts – of men of like faculties and passions with myself, mourning, rejoicing, suffering, triumphing – are but as a *Divina Commedia* of a superhuman (O bear with me, if I say it) Ventriloquist; that the royal Harper, to whom I have so often submitted myself as a *many-stringed instrument* for his fire-tipped fingers to traverse, while every several nerve of emotion, passion, thought, that thrids the flesh and blood of our common humanity, responded to the touch, that this *sweet Psalmist of Israel* was himself as mere an instrument as his harp, an *automaton* poet, mourner, and supplicant; – all is gone, all sympathy, at least, and all example. I listen in awe and fear, but likewise in perplexity and confusion of spirit.

Does not the universally admitted canon – that each part of Scripture must be interpreted by the spirit of the whole – lead to the same practical conclusion as that for which I am now contending; namely, that it is the spirit of the Bible, and not the detached words and sentences, that is infallible and absolute? Practical, I say, and spiritual too; and what knowledge not practical or spiritual are we entitled to seek in our Bibles? Is the grace of God so confined, are the evidences of the present and actuating Spirit so dim and doubtful, that to be assured of the same we must first take for granted that all the life and co-agency of our humanity is miraculously suspended?

Whatever is spiritual is *eo nomine* supernatural; but must it be always and of necessity miraculous? Miracles could open the eyes of the body; and he that was born blind beheld his Redeemer. But miracles, even those of the Redeemer himself, could not open the eyes of the self-blinded, of the Sadducean sensualist or the self-righteous Pharisee; while to have said, *I saw thee under the fig tree*, sufficed to make a Nathanael believe.

No man, I say, can recognize his own inward experiences in such writings, and not find an objectiveness, a confirming and assuring outwardness, and all the main characters of reality, reflected therefrom on the spirit, working in himself and in his own thoughts, emotions, and aspirations – warring against sin, and the motions of sin. The unsubstantial, insulated Self passes away as a stream; but these are the shadows and reflections of the Rock of Ages, and of the Tree of Life that starts forth from its side.

On the other hand, as much of reality, as much of objective truth, as the Scriptures communicate to the subjective experiences of the believer, so much of present life, of living and effective import, do these experiences give to the letter of these Scriptures. In the one *the Spirit itself beareth witness with our spirit*, that we have received the *spirit of adoption*; in the other our spirit bears witness to the power of the Word, that it is indeed the Spirit that proceedeth from God. If in the holy men thus actuated all imperfection of knowledge, all participation in the mistakes and limits of their several ages had been excluded, how could these writings be or become the history and example, the echo and more lustrous image of the work and warfare of the sanctifying Principle in us?

From
Letters, Conversations and Reflections collected by T. Allsop
1836

THE TEACHING PROFESSION

Teachers of youth are, by a necessity of their present condition, either unsound or uncongenial. If they possess that buoyancy of spirit, which best fits them for communicating to those under their charge, the knowledge it is held useful for them to acquire, they are deemed unsound. If they possess a subdued sobriety of disposition, the result of a process compared to which the course of a horse in a mill is positive enjoyment, they of necessity become ungenial. Is this a fitting condition, a meet and just return for the class, Instructors? And yet have I not truly described them? Has any one known a teacher of youth who, having attained any repute as such, has also retained any place in society as an individual? Are not all such men 'Dominic Sampsons' in what relates to their duties, interests, and feelings as citizens; and, with respect to females, do they not all possess a sort of mental odour? Are not all masters, all those who are held in estimation, not scholars, but always masters, even in their sports; and are not the female teachers always teaching and setting right, whilst both not only lose the freshness of youth, both of mind and body, but seem as though they never had been young? They who have to teach can never afford to learn; hence their improgression.

To the above remarks, true as they are in themselves, I am desirous to draw your particular attention. Those who have to teach, a duty which if ably discharged is the highest and most important which society imposes, are placed in a position in which they necessarily acquire a general or generic character, and this, for the most

96

part, unfits them for mixing in society with ease to themselves or to others. Is this just, is it for the advantage of the community that those to whom the highest and most responsible trusts are confided, should be rendered unfit to associate with their fellow men, by something which is imposed upon them, or which they are made to acquire, as teachers? Does not society owe it to this meritorious class, to examine into the causes of these peculiarities with a view to remove ascertained evils, or, by developing them to bring constantly before our eyes the necessity, in their case, of results which at present have such evil influences upon the more genial feelings of so large, and in every way estimable and intelligent a portion of our fellow men. It is requisite that the conviction now become so self-evident, 'that vice is the effect of error and the offspring of surrounding circumstances, the object of condolence and not of anger', should become a habit of the mind in the daily and hourly occurrences of social life. This consummation, so devoutly to be wished, is now for the first time possible; and, when it shall be fully realized, will lead most assuredly to the amelioration of the human race, and whatever has life or is capable of improvement.

FEELING

I devote this brief scroll to Feeling: so no more of disquisition, except it be to declare the entire coincidence of my experience with yours as to the very rare occurrence of strong and deep Feeling in conjunction with free power and vivacity in the expression of it. The most eminent Tragedians, Garrick for instance, are known to have had their emotions as much at command, and almost as much on the surface, as the muscles of their countenances; and the French, who are all actors, are proverbially heartless. Is it that it is a false and feverous state for the centre to live in the circumference? The vital warmth seldom rises to the surface in the form of sensible heat, without becoming hectic and inimical to the life within, the only source of real sensibility. Eloquence itself – I speak of it as habitual and at call – too often is, and is always like to engender, a species of histrionism.

In one of my juvenile poems (on a friend who died in a frenzy fever), you will find that I was jealous of this in myself; and that it is (as I trust it is) otherwise, I attribute mainly to the following causes. A naturally, at once searching and communicative disposition, the necessity of reconciling the restlessness of an ever-working fancy with an intense craving after a resting place for my thoughts in some *principle* that was derived from experience, but of which all other knowledge should be but so many repetitions under various limitations, even as circles, squares, triangles, etc., etc., are but so many positions of space. And, lastly, that my eloquence was most commonly excited by the desire of running away and hiding myself from my personal and inward feelings, *and not for the expression of them*, while doubtless this very effort of feeling gave a passion and glow to my thoughts

> Sloth-jaundiced all! and from my graspless hand
> Drop Friendship's precious pearls, like hour-glass sand.
> I weep, yet stoop not! the faint anguish flows,
> A dreamy pang in Morning's feverish dose.
> Is this piled earth our Being's passless mound?
> Tell me, cold grave! is Death with poppies crowned?
> Tired sentinel! 'mid fitful starts I nod,
> And fain would sleep, though pillowed on a clod.

and language on subjects of a general nature, that they otherwise would not have had. I fled in a circle, still overtaken by the feelings, from which I was ever more fleeing, with my back turned towards them; but above all, my growing deepening conviction of the *transcendency of the moral to the intellectual*, and the inexpressible comfort and inward strength which I experience myself to derive as often as I contemplate truth realized into being by a human will; so that, *as I cannot love without esteem, neither can I esteem without loving*. Hence I *love* but few, but those I love as my own soul; for I feel that without them I should ... not indeed cease to be kind and effluent, but by little and little become a soul-less fixed star, receiving no rays nor influences into my being, *a solitude which I so tremble at, that I cannot attribute it even to the Divine Nature.*

Index of First Lines of Poems

POEMS

Feasts and Fasts
Christina Rossetti

Christina Rossetti (1830–1894) was born in London of Italian parents. With her vivid imagination and innate talent for composing verse, she was an accomplished poet by her late teens. By the mid 1850s her brother Dante Gabriel had become one of the leaders of the Pre-Raphaelite brotherhood, giving Christina the opportunity to publish poetry in the brotherhood's magazine. By 1866 she was established as a leading poet of her day.

Prematurely in 1871 she was stricken with Graves Disease, becoming increasingly preoccupied with the relationship between earth and heaven, life and death. She had inherited a devout Anglican faith from her mother, and from this point on her verse became almost entirely religious. Two of her most religious poems – 'In the Bleak Mid-Winter' and 'Love Came Down at Christmas' – have since been set to music as carols.

This volume focuses on her poetry marking the feasts and fasts of the Christian year. Divided into sections including Advent, Christmas, Lent and Easter, it is designed to be dipped into at the appropriate times, an aid to gentle reflection throughout the year.

POEMS

Emily Brontë

No coward soul is mine
No trembler in the world's storm-troubled sphere
I see Heaven's glories shine
And Faith shines equal arming me from Fear

FROM 'NO COWARD SOUL IS MINE'

Emily Brontë's life is so well known as to need little introduction. She was born in 1818, the daughter of an Anglican parson in Haworth, Yorkshire. Painfully shy but with an extraordinary passion for the moors around her home, she spent most of her life in Haworth. Brief spells at boarding school with her sister Charlotte, as a teacher in Halifax, and as a student in Brussels all ended in homesickness and a desperate longing for the freedom of the moors. She spent the rest of her short life keeping house for her father, dying of tuberculosis in 1848.

Her formative years were dominated by the religious doctrines of her father and her staunchly Methodist aunt. Her spiritual vision, however, transcended formal religion, exalting rather the divine presence within nature. Though her novel *Wuthering Heights* has long been acknowledged as a masterpiece, her poetry has received little attention in its own right. It is, however, profoundly mystical and often breathtaking in its force and intensity. This new selection of her verse seeks to redress the balance.

FOUNT CLASSICS

SONGS AND SERMONS

John Wesley and Charles Wesley

John and Charles Wesley are renowned the world over as joint founders of the Methodist movement. Their teachings have influenced the spiritual lives of millions.

John Wesley (1703–1791) was ordained an Anglican priest. He spent two years in the American colonies, and on his return underwent a transforming spiritual experience. He became a circuit preacher, travelling thousands of miles on horseback to 'spread spiritual holiness through the land'. A highly literate man, he wrote lively treatises including 'A Plain Account of Christian Perfection', in which he reflects on his own spiritual journey. His sermons focus on the central themes of the Gospel and are part of the doctrinal foundation of Methodism.

Charles Wesley (1707–1788) was probably the most gifted of English hymn writers. The first Methodist Hymn Book, edited by John Wesley, was devoted mainly to Charles' hymns. He wrote some nine thousand in all, covering the whole range of Christian worship and including the well-known 'Lo! He Comes with Clouds Descending' and 'Love Divine, All Loves Excelling'. Each one is a masterpiece of scriptural allusion and makes stirring reading.

This selection of the two brothers' liveliest and most accessible writings reveals the influences and beliefs akin to both, and gives vibrant expression to their evangelical faith and experience.

POEMS AND DEVOTIONS

John Donne

John Donne was born in 1572 and, a Roman Catholic in his youth, took Anglican Orders in 1615 and was Dean of St Paul's from 1621 until his death.

His poetry, though forgotten for a long period, is the finest example of the so-called 'metaphysical' style – learned, allusive and witty. It is both highly physical and highly spiritual, with no distinction in method or content between the sacred and secular poems, both of which are included in this anthology.

Less well-known, but equally compelling, are his early *Devotions upon Emergent Occasions*, meditations and prayers issuing from a profound trust in God.

As Dean of St Paul's, Donne gained the reputation of being the finest preacher in the land; his use of strong rhythms and striking images made for powerful sermons. This volume contains edited versions of five of these, including the classic 'Death's Duel'.

THE COMPLETE POEMS

with selected prose
Gerard Manley Hopkins

Gerard Manley Hopkins (1844–1889) was born into a devout Anglican family in Stratford, Essex, and converted to Catholicism in his final year at Oxford. He became a member of the Society of Jesus and was ordained in 1877. After some years as a priest, he became a professor of Classics at University College, Dublin, but died from typhoid four years later at the age of forty-five.

He displayed remarkable poetic creativity throughout his life, though on becoming a Jesuit found this ability difficult to reconcile with religious devotion. Through the teaching of Duns Scotus he came to recognize the importance of allowing individual talent, and hence his poetic gifts, to be exercised in the service of the Church. Sadly, his poetry was rejected for publication in his lifetime, though in later years it was regarded as innovative and highly influential.

Hopkins is best known for his nature mysticism, exploring the revelation of the divine within the natural world. This complete collection of his surviving verse is complemented by a selection of extracts from his notebooks and sermons, specially chosen to reveal the essence of his mystical vision.

TABLE TALK

Martin Luther

Translated by William Hazlitt

Martin Luther (1483–1546) was educated by the Augustian Hermits in Erfurt and at the University of Erfurt, becoming a professor in Wittenberg. He believed in the Pauline principle of justification by faith. This led him to challenge the corruption of the Roman Church – particularly the selling of indulgences – and to become the most famous leader of the Protestant Reformation.

Although Luther published a series of brilliant treatises in 1520, they make fairly heavy reading for the layperson. This volume is a selection of recollections, by friends and family, of things Luther said informally. As a result, it is an easily accessible and personal account of his feelings, ideas and even his humour.

Published here in its famous translation by William Hazlitt, the book celebrates the atmosphere of intellectual and spiritual freedom to be found in Germany at the beginning of the sixteenth century.

JOHN BUNYAN

The Christian
Gordon Wakefield

John Bunyan, born in 1628, son of a Bedford tinker and teenage soldier in the army of Robert Cromwell, fell into a kind of religious madness and emerged from this a soldier in the army of Christ: a fiery preacher in the radical Puritan tradition. His fervour brought him into conflict with the Restoration government, and he spent much time in prison. It was there he wrote his famous masterpiece, *The Pilgrim's Progress*. By the time of his death, he had written some 60 works.

This outstanding biography takes Bunyan seriously as a spiritual guide, and sets his life in the context of the history of English Christianity, as well as the political conflicts of his time.

'Wakefield's excellent book helps us to understand why Bunyan's influence continues down the centuries and across the continents.'

BAPTIST TIMES

'The chief merit of this impressive theological life is to bring back a Bunyan with a vibrant word for *now*, one that leaps all denominational frontiers.'

METHODIST RECORDER

FOUNT CLASSICS

THE PILGRIM'S PROGRESS

John Bunyan

Written in prison, where Bunyan had been sent for unauthorized preaching, and first published in 1678, this classic story has been described as the most popular work of Christian spirituality written in English, and as the first English novel. It describes the road to the Celestial City, by way of Doubting Castle, the Delectable Mountains, Vanity Fair and other places whose names have entered the very fabric of the language.

Fascinating as literature, entertaining as story, profound as spiritual teaching for the soul's journey, *The Pilgrim's Progress* is 'a masterpiece which generation after generation of ordinary men and women have taken to their hearts'.

HUGH ROSS WILLIAMSON

FOUNT CLASSICS

MY CONFESSION

Leo Tolstoy

Leo Tolstoy's literary stature rests almost entirely on his two masterpieces, *Anna Karenina* and *War and Peace*. Less well known are his books on moral and religious themes for which he was dubbed 'the conscience of the continent' in his day. These books were inspired by his mid-life conversion to the Christian faith.

His approach to Christianity was quite distinct. He disliked the dogma, insisting on the simple, practical truths of Jesus' teaching and emphasizing the importance of the individual conscience in upholding these truths. He saw that spiritual insight was often granted to the simple and uneducated in society, prompting a radical change in his own lifestyle.

Written immediately after his conversion and widely praised by his contemporaries, *My Confession* traces the development of Tolstoy's faith and morality. It is an absorbing account of the influences on his life and literature. In a frank, autobiographical style, he reveals the complex intellectual, moral and spiritual turmoil which brought him to the brink of suicide, and the faith through which he eventually attained, to some degree, a peace of mind.

LETTERS OF SPIRITUAL COUNSEL AND GUIDANCE

John Keble

John Keble (1792–1866) possessed an outstanding academic mind, gaining a double first-class Oxford degree when he was 19 and displaying from an early age considerable poetic talent. He was ordained in 1815. His first publication, a book of poetry entitled *The Christian Year*, was so extraordinarily popular that he was rapidly assured of nationwide fame and admiration.

Resisting the trappings of success, he rejected senior posts in the church in favour of life as a rural parish priest in Hursley, Hampshire. He remained, however, very much in the public eye. In 1833, he delivered a controversial sermon condemning political interference in ecclesiastical affairs, on the grounds that the authority of the Church is divinely ordained. He later became adviser to the Tractarian movement, which sought to return the Anglican Church to its Catholic roots. He urged the importance of sacramental confession and encouraged the revival of the daily office.

The letters in this book were collected and first published after Keble's death. During his lifetime he offered sensitive and thoughtful advice in response to many requests for spiritual guidance. He reveals himself to be a man of wisdom and humility, with an innate understanding of the pastoral role.